Differentiating Instruction With Menus

Science

Differentiating Instruction With Menus
Science

Laurie E. Westphal

PRUFROCK PRESS INC.
WACO, TEXAS

Library of Congress Cataloging-in-Publication Data

Westphal, Laurie E., 1967–
  Differentiating instruction with menus. Science / Laurie E. Westphal.
    p. cm.
  Includes bibliographical references.
  ISBN-13: 978-1-59363-227-4 (pbk.)
  ISBN-10: 1-59363-227-4
  1. Science—Study and teaching. 2. Individualized instruction. 3. Curriculum planning. I. Title.
  Q181.W4444 2007
  507.1'2--dc22
                        2007016524

Edited by Jennifer Robins
Production Design by Marjorie Parker

ISBN-13: 978-1-59363-227-4
ISBN-10: 1-59363-227-4

At the time of this book's publication, all facts and figures cited are the most current available; all telephone numbers, addresses, and Web site URLs are accurate and active; all publications, organizations, Web sites, and other resources exist as described in this book; and all have been verified. The authors and Prufrock Press make no warranty or guarantee concerning the information and materials given out by organizations or content found at Web sites, and we are not responsible for any changes that occur after this book's publication. If you find an error or believe that a resource listed here is not as described, please contact Prufrock Press.

Prufrock Press Inc.
P.O. Box 8813
Waco, TX 76714-8813
Phone: (800) 998-2208
Fax: (800) 240-0333
http://www.prufrock.com

CONTENTS

CHAPTER 1

Choice

"Oh my gosh! THAAAAANK YOU!" exclaimed one of my students as he fell to his knees dramatically in the middle of my classroom. I had just had handed out a list menu on the periodic table and told my students they would be able to choose how they wanted to learn the material.

Why Is Choice Important?

Ask adults whether they would prefer to choose what to do or be told what to do, and of course, they are going to say they would prefer to have a choice. Students have the same feelings. Although they may not stand up and demand a choice if none are present, they benefit in many ways from having them.

One benefit of choice is its ability to meet the needs of so many different students and their learning styles. The Dunedin College of Education (Keen, 2001) conducted a research study on the preferred learning styles of 250 gifted students. Students were asked to rank different learning options. Of the 13 different options described to the students, only one option did not receive at least one negative response, and that was the option of having choice. Although all students have different learning styles and preferences, choice is the one option that meets all students' needs. Students are going to choose what best fits their learning styles and educational needs.

> " . . . I am different in the way I do stuff. I like to build stuff with my hands. . . . "
>
> *—Sixth-grade student,*
> *when asked why he enjoyed activities that allow choice.*

Another benefit of choice is a greater sense of independence for the students. What a powerful feeling! Students will be designing and creating a product based on what they envision, rather than what their teacher envisions. When students would enter my middle-school classroom, they often had been trained by previous teachers to produce exactly what the teacher wanted, not what the students thought would be best. Teaching my students that what they envision could be correct (and wonderful) was often a struggle. "Is this what you want?" or "Is this right?" were popular questions as we started the school year. Allowing students to have choices in the products they create to show their learning helps create independence at an early age.

Strengthened student focus on the required content is a third benefit. When students have choices in the activities they wish to complete, they are more focused on the learning that leads to their choice product. Students become excited when they learn information that can help them develop a product they would like to create. Students pay close attention to instruction and have an immediate application for the knowledge being presented in class. Also, if students are focused, they are less likely to be off task during instruction.

Many a great educator has referred to the idea that the best learning takes place when the students have a desire to learn. Some students have a desire to learn anything that is new to them; others do not want to learn anything unless it is of interest to them. By incorporating different activities from which to choose, students stretch beyond what they already know, and teachers create a void that needs to be filled. This void leads to a desire to learn.

How Can Teachers Provide Choices?

> "The GT students seem to get more involved in assignments when they have choice. They have so many creative ideas and the menus give them the opportunity to use them."
>
> —Social studies teacher, when asked how students respond to having choices.

When people go to a restaurant, the common goal is to find something on the menu to satisfy their hunger. Students come into our classrooms having a hunger, as well—a hunger for learning. Choice menus are a way of allowing our students to choose how they would like to satisfy that hunger. At the very least, a menu is a list of choices that students use to choose an activity (or activities) they would like to complete to show what they have learned. At best, it is a complex system in which students earn points by making choices from different areas of study. All menus should also incorporate a free-choice option for those "picky eaters" who would like to make a special order to satisfy their learning hunger.

The next few sections provide examples of the main types of menus that will be used in this book. Each menu has its own benefits, limitations or drawbacks, and time considerations. An explanation of the free-choice option and its management will follow the information on each type of menu.

Tic-Tac-Toe Menu

> "Sometimes I only liked two, but I had to do three."
>
> —Second-grade student, when asked what he liked least about a menu used in his classroom.

Description

The Tic-Tac-Toe Menu (see Figure 1.1) is a basic menu that contains a total of eight predetermined choices and one free choice for students.

All choices are created at the same level of Bloom's Revised taxonomy (Anderson et al., 2001). Each choice carries the same weight for grading and has similar expectations for completion time and effort.

Benefits

Flexibility. This menu can cover one topic in depth, or three different objectives. When this menu covers just one objective, students have the option of completing three projects in a tic-tac-toe pattern, or simply picking three from the menu. When it covers three objectives, students will need to complete a tic-tac-toe pattern (one in each column or row) to be sure they have completed one activity from each objective.

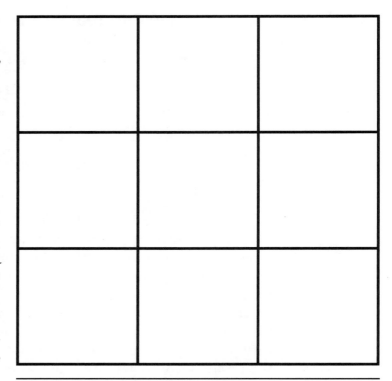

Figure 1.1. Tic-tac-toe menu

Friendly Design. Students quickly understand how to use this menu.

Weighting. All projects are equally weighted, so recording grades and maintaining paperwork is easily accomplished with this menu.

Limitations

Few Topics. These menus only cover one or three topics.

Short Time Period. They are intended for shorter periods of time, between 1–3 weeks.

Student Compromise. Although this menu does allow choice, a student will sometimes have to compromise and complete an activity he or she would not have chosen because it completes the required tic-tac-toe. (This is not always bad, though!)

✔			
✔			
✔			
✔			
✔			
✔			
✔			
✔			
✔			
✔			
✔			

Figure 1.2. List menu

Time Considerations

These menus are usually intended for shorter amounts of completion time—at the most, they should take 3 weeks. If it focuses on one topic in depth, the menu can be completed in one week.

List Menu

Description

The List Menu (see Figure 1.2), or Challenge List, is a more complex menu than the Tic-Tac-Toe Menu, with a total of at least 10 predetermined choices, each with its own point value, and at least one free choice for students. Choices are simply listed with assigned points based on the levels of Bloom's Revised taxonomy. The choices carry different weights and have different expectations for completion time and effort. A point criterion is set forth that equals 100%, and students choose how they wish to attain that point goal.

Benefits

Responsibility. Students have complete control over their grades. They really like the idea that they can guarantee their grade if they complete the required work. If they lose points on one of the chosen assignments, they can complete another to be sure they have met their goal points.

Concept Reinforcement. This menu also allows for an in-depth study of material; however, with the different levels of Bloom's Revised taxonomy being represented, students who are still learning the concepts can choose some of the lower level point value projects to reinforce the basics before jumping into the higher level activities.

Limitations

Few Topics. This menu is best used for one topic in depth, although it can be used for up to three different topics, as well.

Cannot Guarantee Objectives. If it is used for three topics, it is possible for a student to not have to complete an activity for each objective, depending on the choices he or she makes.

Preparation. Teachers need to have all materials ready at the beginning of the unit for students to be able to choose any of the activities on the list, which requires advance planning.

Time Considerations

The List Menus are usually intended for shorter amounts of completion time—at the most, 2 weeks.

2-5-8 Menu

"My favorite menu is the 2-5-8 kind. It's easy to understand and I can pick just what I want to do."
—*Fourth-grade student, when asked about his favorite type of menu.*

Description

A 2-5-8 Menu (see Figure 1.3) is a variation of the List Menu, with a total of at least eight predetermined choices: at least two choices with a point value of two, at least four choices with a point value of five, and at least two choices with a point value of eight. Choices are assigned points based on the levels of Bloom's Revised taxonomy (Anderson et al., 2001). Choices with a point value of two represent the *remember* and *understand* levels, choices with a point value of five represent the *apply* and *analyze* levels, and choices with a point value of eight represent the *evaluate* and *create* levels. All levels of choices carry different weights and have different expectations for completion time and effort.

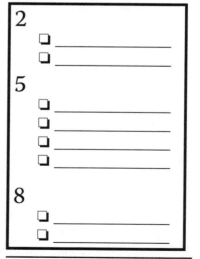

Figure 1.3. 2-5-8 menu

Students are expected to earn 10 points for a 100%. Students choose what combination they would like to use to attain that point goal.

Benefits

Responsibility. With this menu, students still have complete control over their grades.

Guaranteed Activity. This menu's design is also set up in such a way that students must complete at least one activity at a higher level of Bloom's Revised taxonomy in order to reach their point goal.

Limitations

One Topic. Although it can be used for more than one topic, this menu works best with in-depth study of one topic.

No Free Choice. By nature, it does not allow students to propose their own free choice, because point values need to be assigned based on Bloom's Revised taxonomy.

Higher Level Thinking. Students will complete only one activity at a higher level of thinking.

Time Considerations

The 2-5-8 Menus are usually intended for a shorter amount of completion time—at the most, one week.

Baseball Menu

Description

This menu (see Figure 1.4) is a baseball-based variation on the list menu with a total of at least 20 predetermined choices: choices are given values as singles, doubles, triples, or home runs based on the levels of Bloom's taxonomy. Singles represent the *remember* and *understand* levels; doubles, the *apply* and *analyze* levels; triples, the *evaluate* level; and home runs, the *create* level. All levels of choices carry different weights and have different expectations for completion time and effort. Students are expected to earn a certain number of runs (around all four bases) for a 100%. Students choose what combination they would like to use to attain that number of runs.

Benefits

Responsibility. With this menu, students still have complete control over their own grades.

Flexibility. This menu allows for many choices at each level. Students should have no trouble finding something that catches their interest.

Theme. This menu has a fun theme that students enjoy and can be used throughout the classroom. A bulletin board can be set up with a baseball diamond, with each student having his or her own player who can move through the bases. Not only can students keep track of their own RBIs, but they can have a visual reminder of what they have completed, as well.

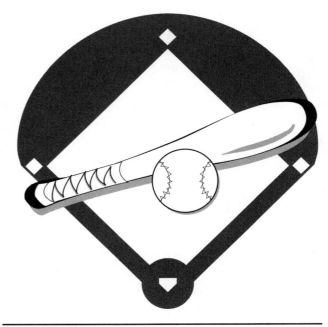

Figure 1.4. Baseball menu

Limitations

One Topic. This menu is best used for one topic with many objectives for in-depth study.

Preparation. With so many choices available to students, teachers should have all materials ready at the beginning of the unit for students to be able to choose any of the activities on the list. This sometimes is a consideration for space in the classroom.

One Free Choice. This menu also has only one opportunity for free choice for students, in the homerun section.

Time Considerations

These menus are usually intended for a longer amount of completion time, depending on the number of runs required for a 100%. At most, these menus are intended for 4 or 5 weeks.

Game Show Menu

> "This menu really challenged my students. If one of my students saw another student choosing a more difficult option, they wanted to choose one, too. I had very few students choose the basic options on this menu. It was wonderful!"
>
> *—Sixth-grade science teacher*

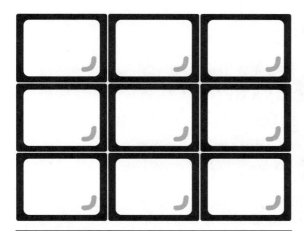

Figure 1.5. Game show menu

Description

The Game Show Menu (see Figure 1.5) is the most complex menu. It covers multiple topics or objectives with at least three predetermined choices and a free student choice for each objective. Choices are assigned points based on the levels of Bloom's taxonomy. All choices carry different weights and have different expectations for completion time and effort. A point criterion is set forth that equals 100%. Students must complete at least one activity from each objective in order to reach their goal.

Benefits

Free Choice. This menu allows many choices for students, but if they do not want to complete the offered activities, they can propose their own activity for each objective.

Responsibility. This menu also allows students to guarantee their own grades.

Different Learning Levels. It also has the flexibility to allow for individualized contracts for different learning levels within the classroom. Each student can contract for a certain number of points for their 100%.

Objectives Guaranteed. The teacher is also guaranteed that the students complete an activity from each objective covered, even if it is at a lower level.

Limitations

Confirm Expectations. The only real limitation here is that students (and parents) must understand the guidelines for completing the menu.

Time Considerations

These menus are usually intended for a longer amount of completion time. Although they can be used as a yearlong menu (each column could be a grading period), they are usually intended for 4–6 weeks.

Free Choice

> " . . . the free choice. I love it, love it!!! I got to do what I really wanted to! [The teacher] let me reserch [sic] my own book."
>
> —*Second-grade student, when asked what she liked most about the menu students had just completed.*

With most of the menus, the students are allowed to submit a free choice for their teacher's consideration. Figure 1.6 shows two sample proposal forms that have been used many times successfully in my classroom. The form used is based on the type of menu being presented. If students are using the Tic-Tac-Toe Menu, there is no need to submit a point proposal. A copy of these forms should be given to each student when each menu is first introduced. A discussion should be held with the students so they understand the expectations of a free choice. If students do not want to make a proposal using the proposal form after the teacher has discussed the entire menu and its activities, they can place the unused form in a designated place in the classroom. Others may want to use their form, and it is often surprising who wants to submit a proposal form after hearing about the opportunity!

Proposal forms must be submitted before students begin working on their free-choice products. The teacher then knows what the students are working on and the student knows the expectations the teacher has for that product. Once approved, the forms can easily be stapled to the student's menu sheet. The students can refer to it as they develop their

Name: _____   Teacher's Approval: _____

Free-Choice Proposal Form for Point-Based Menu

Points Requested: _____   Points Approved: _____

<u>Proposal Outline</u>

1. What specific topic or idea will you learn about?

2. What criteria should be used to grade it? (Neatness, content, creativity, artistic value, etc.)

3. What will your product look like?

4. What materials will you need from the teacher to create this product?

Name: _____   Teacher's Approval: _____

Free-Choice Proposal Form

<u>Proposal Outline</u>

1. What specific topic or idea will you learn about?

2. What criteria should be used to grade it? (Neatness, content, creativity, artistic value, etc.)

3. What will your product look like?

4. What materials will you need from the teacher to create this product?

Figure 1.6. Sample proposal forms for free choice

free-choice product, and when the grading takes place, the teacher can refer to the agreement for the "graded" features of the product.

Each part of the proposal form is important and needs to be discussed with students:

- *Name/Teacher's Approval.* The student must submit this form to the teacher for approval. The teacher will carefully review all of the information, send it back to the student for correction, if needed, and then sign the top.
- *Points Requested.* Found only on the point-based menu proposal form, this is usually where negotiation needs to take place. Students usually will submit their first request for a very high number (even the 100% goal.) They really do equate the amount of time something will take with the amount of points it should earn. But, please note, the points are *always* based on the levels of Bloom's Revised taxonomy. For example, a PowerPoint presentation with a vocabulary word quiz would get minimal points, although it may have taken a long time to create. If the students have not been exposed to the levels of Bloom's Revised taxonomy, this can be difficult to explain. You can always refer to the popular "Bloom's Verbs" to help explain the difference between time requirements and higher level activities.
- *Points Approved.* Found only on the point-based menu proposal form, this is the final decision recorded by the teacher once the point haggling is finished.
- *Proposal Outline.* This is where the student will tell you everything about the product he or she intends to complete. These questions should be completed in such a way that you can really picture what the student is planning on completing. This also shows you that the student knows what he or she is planning on completing.
  - *What specific topic or idea will you learn about?* Students need to be specific here. It is not acceptable to write *science* or *reading*. This is where they look at the objectives of the project and chose which objective their project demonstrates.
  - *What criteria should be used to grade it?* Although there are rubrics for all of the projects that the students might create, it is important for the students to explain what criteria are most important to evaluate the product. The student may indicate that the rubric being used for all the predetermined projects is fine; however, he or she may also want to add other criteria here.
  - *What will your product look like?* It is important that this be as detailed as possible. If a student cannot express what it will "look

like," he or she has probably not given the free-choice plan enough thought.

- *What materials will you need from the teacher to create this product?* This is an important consideration. Sometimes students do not have the means to purchase items for their project. This can be negotiated, as well, but if you ask what students may need, they often will develop even grander ideas for their free choice.

CHAPTER 2

How to Use Menus in the Classroom

There are different ways to use instructional menus in the classroom. In order to decide how to implement each menu, the following questions should be considered: How much prior knowledge of the topic being taught do the students have before the unit or lesson begins and how much information is readily available for students to obtain on their own?

There are three customary ways to use menus in the classroom. Using them for enrichment and supplementary activities is the most common. In this case, the students usually do not have a lot of background knowledge and the information about the topic may not be readily available to all students. The teacher will introduce the menu and the activities at the beginning of a unit. The teacher will then progress through the content at the normal rate, using his or her own curricular materials and periodically allowing class time and homework time throughout the unit for students to work on their menu choices to supplement a deeper understanding of the lessons being taught. This method is very effective, as it builds in an immediate use for the content the teacher is covering. For example, at the beginning of a unit on fractions, the teacher many introduce the menu with the explanation that students may not have all of the knowledge to complete all of their choices yet. During the unit, however, more content will be provided and they will be prepared to work on new choices.

If students want to work ahead, they certainly can find the information on their own, but that is not required. Gifted students often see this as a challenge and will begin to investigate concepts mentioned in the menu before the teacher discusses them. This helps build an immense pool of background knowledge before the topic is even discussed in the classroom. As teachers, we fight the battle of having students read ahead or "come to class prepared to discuss." By introducing a menu at the beginning of a unit and allowing students to complete products as instruction progresses, the students naturally investigate the information and come to class prepared without it being a completely separate requirement.

Another option for using menus in the classroom is to replace certain curricular activities the teacher uses to teach the specified content. In this case, the students may have some limited background knowledge about the content and information is readily available for them in their classroom resources. The teacher would pick and choose which aspects of the content must be directly taught to the students, and which could be appropriately learned and reinforced through product menus. The unit is then designed using both formal instructional lessons and specific menu days where the students will use the menu to reinforce the prior knowledge they already have learned. In order for this option to be effective, the teacher must feel very comfortable with the students' prior knowledge level. Another variation on this method is using the menus to drive center or station activities. Centers have many different functions in the classroom—most importantly reinforcing the instruction that has taken place. Rather than having a set rotation for centers, the teacher could use the menu activities as enrichment or supplementary activities during center time for those students who need more than just reinforcement; centers could be set up with the materials students would need to complete various products.

The third option for menu use is the use of mini-lessons, with the menus driving the accompanying classroom activities. This method is best used when the majority of the students have a lot of prior knowledge about the topic. The teacher can design 10–15 minute mini-lessons, where students would quickly review basic concepts that are already familiar to them. The students are then turned loose to choose an activity on the menu to show they understand the concept. The game show menu usually works very well with this method of instruction, as the topics across the top usually lend themselves to the mini-lessons. It is important that the students have prior knowledge on the content because the lesson cycle is cut very short in this use of menus. Using menus in this way does not allow teachers to use the guided practice step of the lesson, as it is assumed the students already understand the information. The teacher is simply reviewing the information and then moving right to the higher levels of Bloom's Revised taxonomy by asking students to create a product. By using the menus in this way, the teacher avoids the "I already know this" glossy looks from his or her students. Another important consideration is the independence level of the students. In order for this use of menus to be effective, students will need to be able to work independently for up to 30 minutes after the mini-lesson. Because students are often interested in the product they have chosen, this is not a critical issue, but still one worth mentioning as teachers consider how they would like to use various menus in their classroom.

CHAPTER 3

Guidelines for Products

> ". . . each project is unique."
>
> —Fifth-grade student, when asked why he enjoys choice menus.

This chapter outlines the different types of products included in the featured menus, as well as the guidelines and expectations for each. It is very important that students know exactly what the expectations of a completed product are when they choose to work on it. By discussing these expectations *before* students begin and having the information readily available ahead of time, you will limit the frustration on everyone's part.

$1 Contract

Consideration should be given to the cost of creating the products featured on any menu. The resources available to students vary within a classroom, and students should not be graded on the amount of materials they can purchase to make a product look better. These menus are designed to equalize the resources students have available. The materi-

---

$1 Contract

I did not spend more than $1.00 on my _____.

_____   _____
Student Signature   Date

My child, _____, did not spend more than $1.00 on the product he or she created.

_____   _____
Parent Signature   Date

Figure 3.1. $1 contract

als for most products are available for less than a dollar and can often be found in a teacher's classroom as part of the classroom supplies. If a product requires materials from the student, there is a $1 contract as part of the product criteria. This is a very important piece in the explanation of the product. First of all, by limiting the amount of money a child can spend, it creates an equal amount of resources for all students. Second, it actually encourages a more creative product. When students are limited by the amount of materials they can readily purchase, they often have to use materials from home in new and unique ways. Figure 3.1 is a sample of the contract that has been used many times in my classroom with various products.

The Products

Table 3.1 contains a list of the products used in this book. These products were chosen for their flexibility in meeting learning styles, as well as for being products many teachers are already using in their classroom. They have been arranged by learning style—visual, kinesthetic, or auditory—and each menu has been designed to include products from all of the learning styles. Of course, some of the products may be listed in more than one area depending on how they are presented or implemented. The specific expectations for all of the products are presented in an easy-to-

Table 3.1
Products

Visual	Kinesthetic	Auditory
Acrostic	Commercial	Commercial
Advertisement	Concentration Cards	Interview
Book Cover	Diorama	News Report
Brochure/Pamphlet	Flipbook	Play
Cartoon/Comic Strip	Folded Quiz Book	PowerPoint—
Collage	Game	Presentation
Crossword Puzzle	Mobile	Puppet
Greeting Card	Model	Song/Rap
Instruction Card	Play	Speech
Letter	Product Cube	Student-Taught Lesson
Map	Puppet	Video
Mind Map	Science Experiment	You Be the Person
Mural	Student-Taught Lesson	Presentation
Newspaper Article	Three-Dimensional	
Poster	Timeline	
PowerPoint—	Video	
Stand Alone		
Questionnaire		
Recipe/Recipe Card		
Scrapbook		
Story		
Trading Cards		
Venn Diagram		
Video		
Window Pane		
Worksheet		

read card format that can be reproduced for students (see Figure 3.2). This format is convenient for students to have in front of them when they work on their projects. These cards also can be laminated and posted on a bulletin board for easy access during classroom work.

Acrostic	Advertisement	Book Cover
• At least 8.5" x 11" • Neatly written or typed • Target word will be written down the left side of the paper • Each descriptive word chosen must begin with one of the letters from the target word • Each descriptive word chosen must be related to the target word	• At least 8.5" x 11" • A slogan should be included • Color picture of item or service • Include price, if appropriate • Can be developed on the computer	• Front Cover—title, author, and image • Cover Inside Flap—summary of the book • Back Inside Flap—brief biography of the author • Back Cover—editorial comments about the book • Spine—title and author
Brochure/Pamphlet	**Cartoon/Comic Strip**	**Collage**
• At least 8.5" x 11" • Must be in three-fold format; front fold has the title and picture • Must have both pictures and written text • Information should be in paragraph form with at least five facts included	• At least 8.5" x 11" • Should have at least six cells • Must have meaningful dialogue • Must include color	• At least 8.5" x 11" • Pictures must be neatly cut from magazines or newspapers (no clip art) • Label items as required in task
Commercial	**Concentration Cards**	**Crossword Puzzle**
• Must be 5–10 minutes in length • Script must be turned in before commercial is presented • Can be presented live to an audience or recorded • Props or some form of costume must be used • Can include more than one person	• At least 20 index cards (10 matching sets) must be made • Both pictures and words can be used • Information should be placed on just one side of each card • Include an answer key that shows the matches • All cards must be submitted in a carrying bag	• At least 20 significant words or phrases should be included • Develop appropriate clues • Include puzzle and answer key
Diorama	**Flipbook**	**Folded Quiz Book**
• At least 4" x 5" x 8" • Must be self-standing • All interior space must be covered with relevant pictures and information • Name written on the back in permanent ink • Informational/title card attached to diorama	• At least 8.5" x 11" folded in half • All information or opinions are supported by facts • Created with the correct number of flaps cut into the top • Color is optional • Name must be written on the back	• Should be at least 8.5" by 11" folded in half • Should contain at least 10 questions • Created with the correct number of flaps cut into the top • Should have the questions written or typed neatly on upper flaps, and the answers written or typed neatly inside each flap • Color is optional

Figure 3.2. Product guidelines

Game	Greeting Card	Instruction Card
• At least four thematic game pieces • At least 25 colored/thematic squares • At least 20 question/activity cards • Include a thematic title on the board • Include a complete set of rules for playing the game • At least the size of an open file folder (11" x 17")	• Front—colored pictures, words optional • Front Inside—personal note related to topic • Back Inside—greeting or saying; must meet product criteria • Back Outside—logo, publisher, and price for card	• No larger than 5" by 8" • Created on heavy paper or card • Neatly written or typed • Uses color drawings • Provides instructions stated in the task
Interview	**Letter**	**Map**
• Must have at least five questions relevant to the topic begin studied • Questions and answers must be neatly written or typed	• Neatly written or typed • Uses proper letter format • At least three paragraphs in length • Must follow type of letter stated in the menu (e.g., friendly, persuasive, informational)	• At least 8.5" x 11" • Accurate information is included • Includes at least 10 relevant locations • Includes compass rose, legend, scale, and key
Mind Map	**Mobile**	**Mural**
• At least 8.5" x 11" • Must have one central idea • Follow the "no more than four" rule—no more than four words coming from any one word	• At least 10 pieces of related information • Includes color and pictures • Has at least three layers of hanging information • Hangs in a balanced way	• Should be at least 22" x 54" • Must contain at least five pieces of important information • Must have colored pictures • Words are optional, but a title should be included
Model	**News Report**	**Newspaper Article**
• At least 8" x 8" x 12" • Parts of model must be labeled, and should be in scale when appropriate • Must include a title card • Name written on model in ink	• Must address the who, what, where, when, why, and how of the topic • Script of report turned in with project, or before if performance will be "live" • Must be either performed live or recorded	• Must be informational in nature • Must follow standard newspaper format • Must include picture with caption that supports article • At least three paragraphs in length • Neatly written or typed

Figure 3.2. Product guidelines

Play	Poster	PowerPoint—Stand Alone
• Must be between 5–10 minutes long • Script must be turned in before play is presented • Must be presented to an audience • Should have props or some form of costume • Can include more than one person	• Should be the size of a standard poster board • Includes at least five pieces of important information • Must have title • Must contain both words and pictures • Name must be written on the back	• At least 10 informational slides and one title slide with student's name • No more than 15 words per page • Slides must have color and at least one graphic per page • Animation is optional, and should not distract from information being presented
PowerPoint—Presentation	**Product Cube**	**Puppet**
• At least 10 informational slides and one title slide with student's name • No more than 15 words per page • Slides must have color and at least one graphic per page • Animation is optional, and should not distract from information being presented • Presentation should be timed and flow with the oral presentation	• All six sides of the cube must be filled with information • Name must be printed neatly at the bottom of one of the sides of the cube	• Puppet should be handmade and must have a moveable mouth • A list of supplies used to make the puppet must be turned in with the puppet • If used in a play, all play criteria must be met, as well.
Questionnaire	**Recipe/Recipe Card**	**Scrapbook**
• Neatly written or typed • Includes at least 10 questions with possible answers, and at least one question that requires a written response • Questions must be helpful to gathering information on the topic being studied	• Must be written neatly or typed on a piece of paper or an index card • Must have a list of ingredients with measurements for each • Must have numbered steps that explain how to make the recipe	• Cover of scrapbook must have a meaningful title and the student's name • Must have at least five themed pages • Each page will have at least one picture • All photos will have captions
Song/Rap	**Speech**	**Story**
• Words must make sense • Can be presented to an audience or taped • Written words will be turned in before performance or with taped song • Should be at least 2 minutes in length	• Must be at least 2 minutes in length • Should not be read from written paper • Note cards can be used • Written speech must be turned in before speech is presented • Voice must be clear, loud, and easy to understand	• Must be neatly written or typed • Must have all of the elements of a well-written story (setting, characters, problem, events, and solution) • Must be appropriate length to allow for story elements

Figure 3.2. Product guidelines

Three-Dimensional Timeline	Trading Cards	Venn Diagram
• Must be no bigger than a standard-size poster board • Should be divided into equal time units • Must contain at least 10 important dates and have at least two sentences explaining why each date is important • Must have an meaningful, creative object securely attached beside each date to represent that date • Must be able to explain how each object represents each date	• Includes at least 10 cards • Each card should be at least 3" x 5" • Each should have a colored picture • Includes at least three facts on the subject of the card • Cards must have information on both sides • All cards must be submitted in a carrying bag	• At least 8.5" x 11" • Shapes should be thematic and neatly drawn • Must have a title for the entire diagram and a title for each section • Must have at least six items in each section of the diagram • Name must be written on the back of the paper
Video	**Window Pane**	**Worksheet**
• Use VHS or DVD format • Turn in a written plan or storyboard with project • Students will need to arrange their own video recorder or allow teacher at least 3 days notice for use of video recorder • Covers important information about the project • Name must be written on video label	• At least 8.5" x 11" • At least six squares • Each square must include both a picture and words • Name should be recorded on the bottom righthand corner of the front of the window pane	• Must be 8.5" x 11" • Neatly written or typed • Must cover the specific topic or question in detail • Must be creative in design • Must have at least one graphic • An answer key will be turned in with the worksheet
You Be the Person Presentation		
• Take on the role of the person • Cover at least five important facts about his or her life • Presentation should be 3–5 minutes in length • Script must be turned in prior to the presentation • Should be prepared to answer questions from the audience while in character • Must have props or a costume		

Figure 3.2. Product guidelines

CHAPTER 4

Rubrics

"All the grading of the projects kept me from using menus before. The rubric makes it easier though and they [the different projects] are fun to see."

—Fourth-grade teacher,
when asked to explain reservations about using menus.

The most common reason teachers feel uncomfortable with menus is the need for equal grading. Teachers often feel it is easier to grade the same type of product made by all of the students, rather than grading a large number of different products, none of which looks like any other. The great equalizer for hundreds of different products is a generic rubric that can cover all of the important qualities of an excellent product.

All-Purpose Rubric

Figure 4.1 is an example of a rubric that has been classroom tested with various menus. This rubric can be used with any point value activity

Name:_____

All-Purpose Product Rubric

Criteria	Excellent Full Credit	Good Half Credit	Poor No Credit	Self
Content: Is the content of the product well chosen?	Content chosen represents the best choice for the product. Graphics are well chosen and related to content.	Information or graphics are related to content, but are not the best choice for the product.	Information or graphics presented does not appear to be related to topic or task.	
Completeness: Is everything included in the product?	All information needed is included. Product meets the product criteria and the criteria of the task as stated.	Some important information is missing. Product meets the product criteria and the criteria of the task as stated.	Most important information is missing. The product does not meet the task, or does not meet the product criteria.	
Creativity: Is the product original?	Presentation of information is from a new perspective. Graphics are original. Product includes an element of fun and interest.	Presentation of information is from a new perspective. Graphics are not original. Product has elements of fun and interest.	There is no evidence of new thoughts or perspectives in the product.	
Correctness: Is all the information included correct?	All information presented in the product is correct and accurate.	N/A	Any portion of the information presented in the product is incorrect.	
Appropriate Communication: Is the information in the product well communicated?	All information is neat and easy to read. Product is in appropriate format and shows significant effort. Oral presentations are easy to understand and presented with fluency.	Most of the product is neat and easy to read. Product is in appropriate format and shows significant effort. Oral presentations are easy to understand, with some fluency.	The product is not neat and easy to read or the product is not in the appropriate format. It does not show significant effort. Oral presentation was not fluent or easy to understand.	
			Total Grade	

Figure 4.1. All-purpose product rubric

presented in a menu. When a menu is presented to students, this rubric can be reproduced on the back of the menu with its guidelines. It can also be given to students to keep in their folder with their product cards so they always know the expectations as they complete projects throughout the school year. The first time students see this rubric, it should be explained in detail, especially the last column titled *self*. It is very important that students self-evaluate their projects. This column can provide a unique perspective of the project as it is being graded. Note: This rubric was designed to be specific enough that students will know the criteria the teacher is seeking, but general enough that they can still be as creative as they like in the creation of their product.

Student-Taught Lessons and Science Experiment Rubrics

Although the generic rubric can be used for all activities, there are two occasions that seem to warrant a special rubric: student-taught lessons and science experiments. These are both unique situations, with many fine details that must be considered separately.

Teachers often would like to allow students to teach their fellow classmates, but are not comfortable with the grading aspect of the assignment. The student-taught lesson rubric helps focus the student on the important aspects of a well-designed lesson, and also allows teachers to make the evaluation a little more subjective. The student-taught lesson rubric (see Figure 4.2) is appropriate for all levels.

There are two science experiment rubrics, one for more of the elementary expectations found in grades 3–5 (see Figure 4.3), and one for more secondary expectations found in grade 6 and above (see Figure 4.4).

Student-Taught Lesson Grading Rubric   Name _____

Parts of Lesson	Excellent	Good	Fair	Poor	Self
Prepared and Ready: All materials and lesson ready at start of class period, from warm-up to conclusion of lesson.	10 Everything is ready to present.	6 Lesson is present, but small amount of scrambling.	3 Lesson is present, but major scrambling.	0 No lesson ready or missing major components.	
Understanding: Presenter understands the material well. Students understand information presented.	20 Presenter understands; almost all of the students understand information.	12 Presenter understands; 25% of students do not.	4 Presenter understands; 50% of students do not.	0 Presenter is confused.	
Completion: Includes all significant information from section or topic.	15 Includes all important information.	10 Includes most important information.	2 Includes less than 50% of the important information.	0 Information is not related.	
Practice: Includes some way for students to practice or access the information.	20 Practice present, well chosen.	10 Practice present, can be applied effectively.	5 Practice present, not related or best choice.	0 No practice or students are confused.	
Interest/Fun: Most of the class involved, interested, and participating.	15 Everyone interested and participating.	10 75% actively participating.	5 Less than 50% actively participating.	0 Everyone off task.	
Creativity: Information presented in imaginative way.	20 Wow, creative! I never would have thought of that!	12 Good ideas!	5 Some good pieces but general instruction.	0 No creativity; all lecture/ notes/ worksheet.	
				Total Grade:	

Your Topic/Objective:

Comments:

Don't Forget:
All copy requests and material requests must be made at least 24 hours in advance.

Figure 4.2. Student-taught lesson grading rubric

Science Lab Rubric: Grades 3–5

Name: _____

Criteria	Excellent	Good	Fair	Poor	Self
Title: The title is appropriate, represents lab.	**5** Title is appropriate, unique, and represents lab.	**3** Title is present and appropriate, but not unique.	**1** Title is present, but there is no significance to specific lab.	**0** Not present.	
Problem/Purpose: Problem or purpose for experiment clearly stated.	**5** Problem/purpose is present and clearly stated.	**3** Problem/purpose is present and problem/purpose can be understood	**1** Problem/purpose is present, but problem/purpose is not very clear.	**0** Not present.	
Hypothesis: Student states what he or she thinks will be the result of the experiment and why.	**10** Hypothesis is present and tells what is thought and why.	**5** Hypothesis is present and tells what student thought but not why	**3** Hypothesis is present, but student's thoughts are unclear	**0** Not present.	
Materials: All materials present and all exact in description (e.g., "250 ml beaker" rather than "beaker").	**10** All materials present and all exact in description.	**5** Missing no more than one material and all exact in description.	**3** Missing no more than one material and only one is not exact in description.	**0** Missing more than one material and more than one is not exact in description, or materials are not present.	
Procedure: Procedure is in order and easy to read. Written in a way that allows others to repeat the experiment.	**20** Procedure is in order, easy to read, and contains proper punctuation.	**15** Procedure is in order and easy to read, but missing some proper punctuation.	**8** Procedure is not in order or not easy to read and missing some proper punctuation.	**0** Procedure is not in order, easy to read, and missing proper punctuation, or not present.	
Data Table: Data are recorded in an appropriate manner, and are easy to read and understand. Table and data have proper units, titles, and descriptions.	**15** Easy to read, all numbers entered with units, data table has title, columns and rows are labeled.	**10** Easy to read, some data numbers without units, columns and rows are labeled.	**5** Easy to read, columns and rows are not labeled, but can be understood.	**0** Data table is not easy to read, numbers without units, columns and rows are not labeled, or not present	
Representation of Data: Data are recorded in an appropriate manner, and are easy to read and understand. Graph has all proper units, titles, and descriptions.	**15** Easy to read, graphs have units and descriptors, graph has title. Data clearly represented.	**10** Easy to read, graphs have descriptors, but graph has no title or units. Data clearly represented.	**5** Easy to read, graphs have descriptors, but graph has no units or title. Data is not clearly represented.	**0** Not easy to read, graph is missing descriptors, and data is not clearly represented, or not present.	
Conclusion: Conclusion is in paragraph form, revisits hypothesis, explains how the lab was conducted, and suggests a new hypothesis if needed.	**20** Contains proper punctuation and form, describes experiment, and discusses hypothesis and suggests a new one if necessary.	**12** Contains proper punctuation and form and describes experiment, but does not revisit hypothesis or suggest a new one if necessary.	**4** Missing proper punctuation or form and does not revisit hypothesis or suggest a new one if necessary.	**0** Not present.	
				Total Grade:	

Figure 4.3. Science lab rubric: Grades 3–5

Science Lab Rubric: Grade 6 and above   Name: _____

Criteria	Excellent	Good	Fair	Poor	Self
Title: The title is appropriate, represents lab.	**5** Title is appropriate, unique, and represents lab.	**3** Title is present and appropriate, but not unique.	**1** Title is present, but there is no significance to specific lab.	**0** Not present.	
Problem/Purpose: Problem is stated as a question appropriate for the lab. Purpose is stated as a sentence.	**5** Present, proper punctuation and format	**3** Present, proper punctuation, not proper format	**1** Present, not proper format or punctuation	**0** Not present.	
Hypothesis: Hypothesis is stated as an if/then statement and it relates to problem.	**10** Hypothesis is present, contains proper punctuation and format, and relates to problem.	**5** Hypothesis is present, contains proper punctuation, and relates to problem, but not in proper format	**3** Hypothesis is present, but there is no obvious relation to problem, proper punctuation, or proper format.	**0** Not present.	
Materials: All materials present and all exact in description (e.g., "250 ml beaker" rather than "beaker").	**10** All materials present and all exact in description.	**5** Missing no more than one material and all exact in description.	**3** Missing no more than one material and only one is not exact in description.	**0** Missing more than one material and more than one is not exact in description, or materials are not present.	
Procedure: Procedure is sequential and easy to read. Written in a way that would allow others to repeat the experiment. Exact.	**20** Procedure is in order, easy to read, and contains proper punctuation. Exact.	**15** Procedure is in order and easy to read, but missing some proper punctuation. Exact.	**8** Procedure is not in order or not easy to read and missing some proper punctuation. Not exact.	**0** Procedure is not in order or not easy to read, and missing proper punctuation, or not present.	
Data Table: Data are recorded in an appropriate manner, and are easy to read and understand. Table and data have proper units, titles, and descriptions.	**15** Easy to read, all numbers entered with units, data table has title, columns and rows are labeled.	**10** Easy to read, some data numbers without units, columns and rows are labeled.	**5** Easy to read, columns and rows are not labeled, but can be understood.	**0** Data table is not easy to read, numbers without units, columns and rows are not labeled, or not present	
Representation of Data: Data are recorded in an appropriate manner, and are easy to read and understand. Graph has all proper units, titles, and descriptions.	**15** Easy to read, graphs have units and descriptors, graph has title. Data clearly represented.	**10** Easy to read, graphs have descriptors, but graph has no title or units. Data clearly represented.	**5** Easy to read, graphs have descriptors, but graph has no units or title. Data is not clearly represented.	**0** Not easy to read, graph is missing descriptors, and data is not clearly represented, or not present.	
Conclusion: Conclusion is in paragraph form, revisits hypothesis, explains how the lab was conducted, discusses possible errors, and suggests a new hypothesis if needed.	**20** Contains proper punctuation and form, describes experiment, discusses possible errors, and discusses hypothesis and suggests a new one if necessary.	**12** Contains proper punctuation and form, describes experiment, and discusses hypothesis and suggests a new one if necessary, but does not discuss possible errors.	**4** Missing proper punctuation or form, or revisits hypothesis but does not suggest a new one if necessary.	**0** Does not revisit hypothesis or conclusion, or not present.	
				Total Grade:	

Figure 3.4. Science lab rubric: Grade 6 and above

The Menus

How to Use the Menu Pages

Each menu in this section has:
- an introduction page for the teacher,
- the content menu,
- any specific guidelines, and
- activities mentioned in the menu.

Introduction Pages

The introduction pages are meant to provide an overview of each menu. They are divided into five areas.

1. *Objectives covered through the menu and activities.* This area will list all of the objectives that the menu can address. Menus are arranged in such a way that if students complete the guidelines set forth in the instructions for the menu, all of these objectives will be covered.

2. *Materials needed by students for completion.* For each menu, it is expected that the teacher will provide or students will have access to the following materials: lined paper; glue; crayons, colored pencils,

or markers; and blank 8 ½" by 11" white paper. The introduction page also includes a list of additional materials that may be needed by students. Students do have the choice about the menu items they can complete, so it is possible that the teacher will not need all of these materials for every student.

3. *Special notes.* Some menus allow students to choose to present demonstrations, experiments, songs, or PowerPoint presentations to their classmates. This section will give any special tips on managing these student presentations. This section will also share any tips to consider for a specific activity.

4. *Time frame.* Most menus are best used in at least a one-week time frame. Some are better suited to more than 2 weeks. This section will give you an overview about the best time frame for completing the entire menu, as well as options for shorter time periods. If teachers do not have time to devote to an entire menu, they can certainly choose the 1–2-day option for any menu topic students are currently studying.

5. *Suggested forms.* This is a list of the rubrics that should be available for students as the menus are introduced. If a menu has a free-choice option, the appropriate proposal form also will be listed here.

CHAPTER 5

Physical Science

States of Matter

Tic-Tac-Toe Menu

Objectives Covered Through This Menu and These Activities
- Students will identify the three states of matter.
- Students will state properties of each of state of matter.
- Students will classify substances as different states of matter.
- Students will identify how substances change from one state to another.

Materials Needed by Students for Completion
- Coat hangers (for mobile)
- Index cards (for mobile)
- String (for mobile)
- Rulers (for cartoon)
- Socks (for puppets)
- Paper bags (for puppets)
- Magazines (for collage)
- Microsoft PowerPoint or other slideshow software

Special Notes on the Use of This Menu
This menu gives students the option to create a puppet show. This will take some class time for students to present. It is often best to set a date for any presentations that will be made when the menu is first given to students so they are aware of when they will present their products if they choose to do a presentation.

Time Frame
- 2 weeks—Students are given the menu as the unit is started. As the teacher presents lessons throughout the week, he or she should refer back to the options associated with that content. The teacher will go over all of the options for that content and have students place checkmarks in the boxes that represent the activities they are most interested in completing. As teaching continues over the next 2 weeks, activities chosen and completed should make a column or a row. When students complete this pattern, they will have completed one activity from three different objectives.
- 1 week—At the start of the unit, the teacher chooses the three activities he or she feels are most valuable for the students. Stations can be

set up in the classroom. These three activities are available for student choice throughout the week, as regular instruction takes place.

- 1–2 days—The teacher chooses an activity from the menu to use with the entire class.

Suggested Forms

- All-purpose rubric

The Three States of Matter

☐ *Make a Mobile* There are examples of the three states of matter all around us. Make a mobile that shows the three states of matter and the properties of each. Provide an example of each state of matter.	☐ *Create a Cartoon* Think about the properties of gasses. Create a cartoon about a super hero with gas-like properties and his adventures on a very busy day.	☐ *Write a Story* Matter changes continuously on earth. Write a story about a liquid that always wanted to be a solid. Discuss his or her journey and how this goal was reached.
☐ *Design Puppets* Design puppets for a puppet show depicting a soap opera that has the three states of matter as the main characters. Be creative in naming the soap opera and the characters, as well as in designing the puppets.	☐ *Free Choice* (Fill out your proposal form before beginning the free choice!)	☐ *Develop a Brochure* Water is the most common liquid both on the earth and in our bodies. Develop a brochure about water, its properties, and its value to us.
☐ *Design a PowerPoint Presentation* Design a PowerPoint presentation on solids, liquids, and gasses. Include detailed information on the properties of each, as well as examples.	☐ *Conduct an Interview* Conduct a make-believe interview with an important gas. What would you like to know? Write the questions, as well as the responses you might hear during the interview.	☐ *Create a Collage* Think about all of the different states of matter you see in an average day. Create a collage with at least six pictures of each state of matter. Label each picture with its state.

Check the boxes you plan to complete. They should form a tic-tac-toe across or down.
All products are due by: _____.

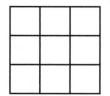

Physical Properties of Matter

Tic-Tac-Toe Menu

Objectives Covered Through This Menu and These Activities

- Students will use a thermometer to measure temperature.
- Students will explain what happens to the particles of a material as the temperature increases.
- Students will understand the concept of buoyancy.
- Students will test the buoyancy of everyday items.
- Students will understand what a conductor is and how to test for the strength of a conductor.
- Students will use a balance to measure mass.
- Students will use a graduated cylinder to measure volume.
- Students will calculate density from the mass and volume of everyday objects.

Materials Needed by Students for Completion

- Thermometer
- Balance
- Graduated cylinder
- Calculator
- Poster board or large white paper
- Materials for student-created models (e.g., marbles, BB shot, ping-pong balls, petri dishes)
- Materials for buoyancy experiment (e.g., household items, large container for water)
- Materials for conductor tester (e.g., wire, light bulbs, batteries)

Time Frame

- 2 weeks—Students are given the menu as the unit is started. As the teacher presents lessons throughout the week, he or she should refer back to the options associated with that content. The teacher will go over all of the options for that content and have students place checkmarks in the boxes that represent the activities they are most interested in completing. As teaching continues over the next 2 weeks, activities chosen and completed should make a column or a row. When students complete this pattern, they will have completed one activity from three different objectives.

- 1 week—At the start of the unit, the teacher chooses the three activities he or she feels are most valuable for the students. Stations can be set up in the classroom. These three activities are available for student choice throughout the week, as regular instruction takes place.
- 1–2 days—The teacher chooses an activity from the menu to use with the entire class.

Suggested Forms

- Lab report rubric
- All-purpose rubric
- Proposal form

Name:_____

Physical Properties of Matter

☐ *Temperature* Develop a worksheet that focuses on reading a thermometer. Include two different temperature scales and have at least five questions with examples. Give your worksheet to one of your classmates to fill out.	☐ *Buoyancy* Design an experiment that will test the buoyancy of 10 household objects. Conduct the experiment and record all of the information on a lab report.	☐ *Conduction* Research what property of conductors allows electricity to pass through them quickly. Create a model to show this property of conductors and what happens when electricity passes through them.
☐ *Conduction* Develop an instrument that can test if an object is a conductor or an insulator. Test 10 household objects. Record your findings in a lab report format.	☐ **Free Choice** (Fill out your proposal form before beginning the free choice!)	☐ *Temperature* Select four locations in your school. Record the temperature at each location for one week. Compare your results after a week. Draw conclusions about the temperature differences between locations, as well as between days of the week and write your results in paragraph form.
☐ *Density* Choose five objects from your classroom. Make a data table to record the mass and the volume of each object. Calculate the objects' density. Rank the items from least to most dense.	☐ *Temperature* Temperature affects the particles of a substance. Create a model that can show what happens to a substance's particles as it heats from a solid to a gas.	☐ *Mass* Make a "how-to" poster that explains how to use a balance correctly. Show how to measure the mass of a pencil or another common object as your example.

Check the boxes you plan to complete. They should form a tic-tac-toe across or down. All products are due by: _____.

Mixtures and Compounds

2-5-8 Menu

Objectives Covered Through This Menu and These Activities

- Students will define mixtures and compounds.
- Students will categorize mixtures and compounds.
- Students will identify properties of mixtures and compounds.
- Students will identify mixtures and compounds in their daily lives.

Materials Needed by Students for Completion

- Magazines (for collage)
- Video camera
- Materials for student-created experiment
- Mixture and Compound Lab instruction sheet
- Magnet and hand lens (for mixture lab)
- 10 closable bags (for mixture lab)
- Flour (for mixture lab bag 1)
- Sandy soil (for mixture lab bag 2)
- Cereal mix (for mixture lab bag 3)
- Chocolate peanut candies (for mixture lab bag 4)
- Cornstarch (for mixture lab bag 5)
- Iron filings and pepper (for mixture lab bag 6)
- Oil and colored water (for mixture lab bag 7)
- Uncooked pasta noodles (for mixture lab bag 8)
- Sand and sugar (for mixture lab bag 9)
- Chocolate chips (for mixture lab bag 10)

Special Notes on the Use of This Menu

This menu does allow students the option to share with the class their examples of mixtures and compounds, as well as present an experiment to their classmates. This will take some class time for students to complete. It is often best to set up one day for the presentation of their examples, and one day for experiments. Choose days that would best reinforce your instruction. Rather than having these student presentations add to your present teaching, have them replace part of what you would normally present. This menu also has a mixture investigation that is set up to be a bucket lab. The teacher can easily make two sets of the materials and have them available for students to use in their free time.

Time Frame

- 1–2 weeks—Students are given the menu as the unit is started, and the teacher discusses all of the product options on the menu. As the different options are discussed, students will choose products that add to a total of 10 points. As the lessons progress through the week, the teacher and students refer back to the options associated with the content being taught.
- 1–2 days—The teacher chooses an activity from the menu to use with the entire class.

Suggested Forms

- Lab report rubric
- All-purpose rubric
- Proposal form for point-based projects

Name:_____

Mixtures and Compounds

Directions: Choose two activities from the menu below. The activities must total 10 points. Place a checkmark next to each box to show which activities you will complete. All activities must be completed by

_____.

---

2 Points

❏ Create a mind map for mixtures and compounds.

❏ Collect 10 items from home; five should be examples of mixtures, and five should be compounds. Bring your collection to class to share.

---

5 Points

❏ Find a recipe for an edible mixture and an edible solution. Prepare each and bring samples for the class. Be ready to explain why each is a mixture or solution during the taste testing.

❏ Complete the Mixture Lab.

❏ Collect various pictures of mixtures and compounds found in our daily lives. Make a collage with the pictures; label the mixtures and compounds in the collage.

❏ Free choice—Prepare a proposal form and submit it to your teacher for approval.

---

8 Points

❏ Design an experiment for the class in which your classmates will determine if a substance is a mixture or a compound. Submit your lab report before presenting your experiment to the class.

❏ Make an educational science video on mixtures and compounds. You get to be the science host, so be creative!

Mixture and Compound Lab

Research—Using reference materials, locate the definition of *mixtures* and *compounds*. Record your findings.

Problem—How can you identify mixtures and compounds?

Materials—10 baggies containing the substances prepared by your teacher, magnet, and hand lens

Procedure

1. Examine the contents of each labeled bag. If contents are difficult to see, use the hand lens.
2. Record a description of the bag's content in the data table below.
3. Based on your research about the definition of mixtures and compounds, record whether you think each bag is a mixture or a compound.
4. Lastly, defend the choice you made for each item.

Data Table

Bag Number	Description of Contents	Mixture or Compound	Defense
1			
2			
3			
4			
5			
6			
7			
8			
9			
10			

Questions

1. What is an easy way to distinguish a compound from a mixture?

2. What are three mixtures you see on a daily basis?

3. What are three compounds you can find in the classroom?

4. How do compounds affect our daily lives?

Conclusion—Write a brief conclusion that states what you have learned about mixtures and compounds and their identification.

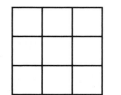

Simple Machines

Tic-Tac-Toe Menu

Objectives Covered Through This Menu and These Activities

- Students will identify the six different types of simple machines.
- Students will understand that compound machines are made of simple machines.
- Students will investigate the history behind simple machines and their discovery.
- Students will give examples of the different types of simple machines.

Materials Needed by Students for Completion

- Poster board or large white paper
- Magazines (with pictures of simple machines)
- Coat hangers (for mobile)
- Index cards (for mobile)
- String (for mobile)
- Various household simple machines

Special Notes on the Use of This Menu

This menu does give students the option to create an original song or rap to help remember the different type of simple machines. This will take some class time for students to present. It is often best to set a date for any presentations that will be made when the menu is first given to students so they are aware of when they will present their song or rap if they choose to do this presentation. Allowing students to teach their classmates the songs will help everyone remember the simple machines.

Time Frame

- 2 weeks—Students are given the menu as the unit is started. As the teacher presents lessons throughout the week, he or she should refer back to the options associated with that content. The teacher will go over all of the options for that content and have students place checkmarks in the boxes that represent the activities they are most interested in completing. As teaching continues over the next 2 weeks, activities chosen and completed should make a column or a row. When students complete this pattern, they will have completed one activity from three different objectives.

- 1 week—At the start of the unit, the teacher chooses the three activities he or she feels are most valuable for the students. Stations can be set up in the classroom. These three activities are available for student choice throughout the week, as regular instruction takes place.
- 1–2 days—The teacher chooses an activity from the menu to use with the entire class.

Suggested Forms

- All-purpose rubric
- Proposal forms

Name:_____

Simple Machines

☐ *Write a Story* Simple machines were used by the Greeks to do work in their daily lives. Pretend you are a Greek worker who uses levers and screws to get your job done. Write a story about a day at work.	☐ *Invent a Machine* Complex machines are made from many simple machines. Invent a complex machine by using at least five simple machines. Draw the compound machine and explain how each simple machine helps the complex machine do its work.	☐ *Make a Mobile* There are six different types of simple machines. Make a mobile of these six types of simple machines with examples and pictures of each.
☐ *Prepare a Flipbook* Prepare a flipbook of six simple machines. Write a simple machine on each flap. Order the machines from most important to least important based on your opinion. On each flap, include examples of each machine and why that type of machine is important to humans.	☐ **Free Choice** (Fill out your proposal form before beginning the free choice!)	☐ *Keep a Journal* Keep a simple machine journal for 24 hours. Record every machine you use for 24 hours. (Compound machines should be broken down into simple machines to the best of your ability.)
☐ *Dissect a Picture* Find a picture of a compound machine. Identify and label all of the simple machines that help the compound machine do its work.	☐ *Create a Song* Students sometimes have trouble remembering the different types of simple machines. Create a song or rap to help you remember all six types of simple machines. Teach your song to the class.	☐ *Make a Poster* Archimedes is famous for his development and work with simple machines. Create a poster about Archimedes and his discoveries.

Check the boxes you plan to complete. They should form a tic-tac-toe across or down. All products are due by: _____.

Sound and Vibrations

2-5-8 Menu

Objectives Covered Through This Menu and These Activities

- Students will describe how various objects create sound.
- Students will understand that vibrations create sound.
- Students will create sounds from different household objects.
- Students will understand that sound travels at different speeds through different materials.
- Students will distinguish between sound and pitch.
- Students will describe how different instruments produce different pitches.

Materials Needed by Students for Completion

- Poster board or large white paper
- Toot a Flute activity page
- Materials for student-created experiment
- Recycled materials for building a musical instrument

Special Notes on the Use of This Menu

This menu offers students the option to build their own musical instrument that they will present to the class. Students will discuss how their instrument creates sounds and play an identifiable song. Each presentation should only take about 3–4 minutes.

Time Frame

- 1–2 weeks—Students are given the menu as the unit is started, and the teacher discusses all of the product options on the menu. As the different options are discussed, students will choose products that add to a total of 10 points. As the lessons progress through the week, the teacher and students refer back to the options associated with the content being taught.
- 1–2 days—The teacher chooses an activity from the menu to use with the entire class.

Suggested Forms

- Lab report rubric
- All-purpose rubric

Name:_____

Sound and Vibrations

Directions: Choose two activities from the menu below. The activities must total 10 points. Place a checkmark next to each box to show which activities you will complete. All activities must be completed by

_____.

2 Points

❒ Make a poster that shows how sounds are produced. Show at least three examples on your poster (including the vocal cords).

❒ Choose a common musical instrument and research how it creates its sounds and different pitches. Create an informational pamphlet about the instrument to share with other students.

5 Points

❒ Complete the Toot a Flute activity and submit a lab report for the activity.

❒ Collect six items from home that can be used to create vibrations or sounds. Demonstrate your items for the class and explain how each one creates sound.

❒ Make an advertisement for a new soundproofing material. It should include the composition of the new material and how it helps stop sound.

❒ Make a working model that shows how sound travels at different speeds through solids, liquids, and gasses.

8 Points

❒ Build your own musical instrument from recycled materials. You should be able to play a simple recognizable tune on your instrument for the class. Be ready to explain how your instrument creates sound and pitch.

❒ Develop an experiment with a lab report that tests how the speed of sound travels through solids, liquids, and gasses.

Toot a Flute

Purpose—The purpose of this activity is to explore how sound is produced and determine what causes changes in pitch.

Materials—2 drinking straws and a pair of scissors for each student

Procedures

1. Flatten one end of one of your straws by chewing on it.

2. Cut the flattened end on the straw into a V-shape for your mouthpiece.

3. Blow hard on the flattened end of the flute.

4. Record a description of the sound you created.

5. You can create different sounds or pitches by varying the length of the straw. Create a data chart on your own paper to record your observations as you shorten the straw.

6. Slowly shorten the straw by cutting off small sections from the open end using your scissors.

7. Record the changes in pitch that you hear in your data table.

8. Throw away what is left of your small flute and all of the pieces of straw that you have cut off.

9. When you used the first straw, you varied the pitch by shortening the straw with your scissors. You can also vary the pitch by varying the length of air within the straw. Using the other straw, flatten the end and cut to create a mouthpiece.

10. Instead of shortening the straw with scissors, this time you will cut small holes along the length of the straw so it resembles a flute. Experiment with your finger placements to create different pitches.

11. Draw a diagram that shows the locations of your holes and what changes these holes create in pitch.

12. Write a paragraph to conclude your activity. This paragraph should summarize the activity, explain how sound is created, and describe what affects the pitch of musical instrument.

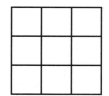

Light and Its Properties

Tic-Tac-Toe Menu

Objectives Covered Through This Menu and These Activities

- Students will define *transparent*, *translucent*, and *opaque*.
- Students will categorize materials as transparent, translucent, and opaque.
- Students will investigate reflection and refraction.
- Students will investigate the working of optical instruments such as a camera, telescope, prism, kaleidoscope, and eyeglasses.
- Students will research how optical instruments were developed.

Materials Needed by Students for Completion

- Poster board or large white paper
- Build a Kaleidoscope activity page
- Kaleidoscope materials
- Materials for building a reflecting telescope (e.g., mirrors, toilet paper tubes, etc.)

Special Notes on the Use of This Menu

This menu allows students to present or share three different products: how an optical instrument uses light, an optical instrument, or a sculpture made of light transmitting materials. Each presentation should take less than 5 minutes, but they all create teachable moments for the teacher. Plan on having the sculpture presentations on the day after you have discussed transparent, translucent, and opaque materials as a quick warm-up or review of the concepts. The instrument presentations can be presented in one day or could be spread out throughout the unit.

Time Frame

- 2 weeks—Students are given the menu as the unit is started. As the teacher presents lessons throughout the week, he or she should refer back to the options associated with that content. The teacher will go over all of the options for that content and have students place checkmarks in the boxes that represent the activities they are most interested in completing. As teaching continues over the next 2 weeks, activities chosen and completed should make a column or a row. When students complete this pattern, they will have completed one activity from three different objectives.

- 1 week—At the start of the unit, the teacher chooses the three activities he or she feels are most valuable for the students. Stations can be set up in the classroom. These three activities are available for student choice throughout the week, as regular instruction takes place.
- 1–2 days—The teacher chooses an activity from the menu to use with the entire class.

Suggested Forms

- All-purpose rubric
- Proposal forms

Name:_____

Light and Its Properties

☐ *Light and Materials* Design an acrostic for the terms *opaque, transparent,* and *translucent.* Record an example for each letter of the three words.	☐ *Light Experiments* Complete the Build a Kaleidoscope activity.	☐ *Optical Instruments* Demonstrate how one of the following optical instruments uses light: camera, telescope, or eyeglasses for nearsighted and farsighted people.
☐ *Optical Instruments* Build a working reflecting telescope or simple camera. Be prepared to demonstrate your instrument and include directions for the construction of the instrument written in your own words.	☐ **Free Choice** (Fill out your proposal form before beginning the free choice!)	☐ *Light Experiments* Using a prism, write and conduct an experiment that proves that white light is made of the other colors of light.
☐ *Light Experiments* Choose four objects from your classroom. Predict how you think each will look when placed in the water. Place each into a container of water. Fold a piece of paper into four and draw what each object looked like.	☐ *Optical Instruments* Show how the first camera or microscope was developed. Write a report or create a poster with the information you discovered.	☐ *Light and Materials* Collect different examples of transparent, translucent, and opaque materials. Create a modern art sculpture using the items you collected. Share your sculpture with the class.

Check the boxes you plan to complete. They should form a tic-tac-toe across or down. All products are due by: _____.

Build a Kaleidoscope

Purpose—In this activity, you will build a simple kaleidoscope.

Materials—2 black film canisters, one with the bottom removed; a hammer; a nail; plastic wrap; small plastic beads; 3 plastic microscope slides; black electrical tape; rubber band; and scissors

Procedures
1. Have your teacher help you make a hole in the bottom of the black film canister using the hammer and nail. This will become the eyehole of the kaleidoscope that you will look through.
2. Place the three microscope slides down on the desk so their edges almost touch. Tape the slides together along their long edges.
3. Turn the slides over so the sides are tape side down and bring up the ends of the slides to form a triangle shape.
4. Tape along the long edge so the slides form a triangular-shaped prism.
5. Very carefully, insert the three plastic microscope slides into the film canister. They will stick out a little bit.
6. Place the other film canister over the microscope slides that are sticking out. Using the black tape, tape the two film canisters together.
7. Cut two pieces of plastic wrap that are approximately 6 centimeters by 6 centimeters.
8. Put one piece of plastic wrap down and choose a few small beads to place in the center for your kaleidoscope.
9. Place the other piece of plastic wrap on top of the beads. Gather the two layers and attach them to the open end of the film canister with the rubber band.
10. By turning the kaleidoscope, you will see different patterns inside.

Questions
1. Is this an example of reflection or refraction? How do you know?
2. Where else have you seen light used this way?

Conclusion—Write a brief conclusion that states how you built your kaleidoscope, as well as how the kaleidoscope shows the properties of light.

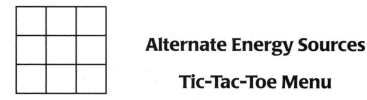

Alternate Energy Sources

Tic-Tac-Toe Menu

Objectives Covered Through This Menu and These Activities
- Students will identify the different types of alternate energy sources: solar, wind, hydrothermal, nuclear, and geothermal.
- Students will discuss the advantages and disadvantages of fossil fuels, as well as alternate energy sources.
- Students will show how a nuclear power plant creates energy.
- Students will demonstrate how a hydroelectric plant creates energy.

Materials Needed by Students for Completion
- Poster board or large white paper
- Microsoft PowerPoint or other slideshow software
- Graph paper or Internet access (for crossword puzzle)
- Materials for demonstrations

Time Frame
- 2 weeks—Students are given the menu as the unit is started. As the teacher presents lessons throughout the week, he or she should refer back to the options associated with that content. The teacher will go over all of the options for that content and have students place checkmarks in the boxes that represent the activities they are most interested in completing. As teaching continues over the next 2 weeks, activities chosen and completed should make a column or a row. When students complete this pattern, they will have completed one activity from three different objectives.
- 1 week—At the start of the unit, the teacher chooses the three activities he or she feels are most valuable for the students. Stations can be set up in the classroom. These three activities are available for student choice throughout the week, as regular instruction takes place.
- 1–2 days—The teacher chooses an activity from the menu to use with the entire class.

Suggested Forms
- All-purpose rubric
- Proposal forms

Alternate Energy Sources

☐ *Prepare a News Report*	☐ *Construct a Model*	☐ *Prepare a Report*
Your city is thinking about changing from fossil fuels to another course of energy. Which alternate source would be the best? Why? Include the advantages and disadvantages of your choice in your news report.	Design a working model that shows how wind energy can be converted into electrical energy.	Research common alternate energy sources. Which of these are most commonly used in your state? Explain why this may be most common. Present all of the information gathered in a report.
☐ *Create a Crossword Puzzle*	☐ *Free Choice* (Fill out your proposal form before beginning the free choice!)	☐ *Make a Poster*
Think about all of the different types of energy sources. Create a crossword puzzle containing the significant vocabulary words related to the different types of energy sources.		Make a poster that shows how a nuclear power plant creates energy.
☐ *Create a Demonstration*	☐ *Design a PowerPoint Presentation*	☐ *Write a Paper*
Hydroelectric plants create energy by using the energy in running water. Create a demonstration for the class that shows how a hydroelectric plant creates energy.	Make a PowerPoint presentation about the different alternate energy sources. Include advantages and disadvantages for each type.	Get ready for a debate. Which energy source would you prefer in your neighborhood: wind, solar, or nuclear? Write a paper with your decision. Be sure and think about costs, space, dangers, and the like.

Check the boxes you plan to complete. They should form a tic-tac-toe across or down. All products are due by: _____.

CHAPTER 6

Biological Science

```
2
  □ ___ ___
5
  □ ___ ___
  □ ___ ___
  □ ___ ___
8
  □ ___ ___
```

Plants

2-5-8 Menu

Objectives Covered Through This Menu and These Activities

- Students will identify the parts of flowering plants including the parts of the flowers.
- Students will identify the stages of a plant life cycle.
- Students will distinguish between flowering plants and conifers.
- Students will classify plants and leaves as monocots and dicots.

Materials Needed by Students for Completion

- Poster board or large white paper
- Graph paper or Internet access (for crossword puzzle)
- Microsoft PowerPoint or other slideshow software
- Various materials for class lesson on plants

Special Notes on the Use of This Menu

This menu gives students the choice to present a lesson to the class. Students should turn in their lesson plan to the teacher before they make their presentation. In this case, this short lesson could replace a lesson the teacher had planned on teaching.

Time Frame

- 1–2 weeks—Students are given the menu as the unit is started, and the teacher discusses all of the product options on the menu. As the different options are discussed, students will choose products that add to a total of 10 points. As the lessons progress through the week, the teacher and students refer back to the options associated with the content being taught.
- 1–2 days—The teacher chooses an activity from the menu to use with the entire class.

Suggested Forms

- All-purpose rubric
- Student-taught lesson rubric

Name:_____

Plants

Directions: Choose two activities from the menu below. The activities must total 10 points. Place a checkmark next to each box to show which activities you will complete. All activities must be completed by _____.

2 Points

❑ Make a poster of a complete flower. Label the five parts and record an explanation of the function of each.

❑ Construct a crossword puzzle about leaves, plants, the parts of a flower, and the life cycle of a plant.

5 Points

❑ Make a plant identification brochure. It should discuss how to identify monocots and dicots, as well as how to distinguish flowering plants from conifers if no flowers or cones are present.

❑ Create a Venn diagram to compare and contrast flowering plants and conifers.

❑ Design a PowerPoint game based on the information presented about plants. It must have at least 20 questions for your classmates to answer.

❑ Create a leaf collection book. Collect 10 different leaves, and record where each leaf was found. Using reference materials, classify each as a monocot or a dicot.

8 Points

❑ Write and perform a play depicting a myth that explains how the parts of the plant and flower got their names. Be creative!

❑ Design and teach a class lesson on what interests you most about the study of plants. The lesson should include why you chose these concepts to share with the class. Prepare a handout or activity for your classmates based on your lesson.

Food Chains

2-5-8 Menu

Objectives Covered Through This Menu and These Activities

- Students will categorize producers, consumers, and decomposers.
- Students will identify local food chains or food webs.
- Students will identify living and nonliving components of a food web.
- Students will understand how energy moves through a food chain.
- Students will understand that all parts of a cycle are important and will make predictions about the consequences of removing one part.
- Students will identify factors that can change food webs.

Materials Needed by Students for Completion

- Blank index cards (for card game)
- Shoe boxes (for dioramas)
- Microsoft PowerPoint or other slideshow software
- Materials for student-taught lesson on Energy in Food Chains

Special Notes on the Use of This Menu

This menu gives students the choice to present a lesson to the class. Students should turn in their lesson plan to the teacher before they make their presentation. In this case, this short lesson could replace a lesson the teacher had planned on teaching.

Time Frame

- 1–2 weeks—Students are given the menu as the unit is started, and the teacher discusses all of the product options on the menu. As the different options are discussed, students will choose products that add to a total of 10 points. As the lessons progress through the week, the teacher and students refer back to the options associated with the content being taught.
- 1–2 days—The teacher chooses an activity from the menu to use with the entire class.

Suggested Forms

- All-purpose rubric
- Student-taught lesson rubric
- Proposal form for point-based projects

Name:_____

Food Chains

Directions: Choose two activities from the menu below. The activities must total 10 points. Place a checkmark next to each box to show which activities you will complete. All activities must be completed by _____.

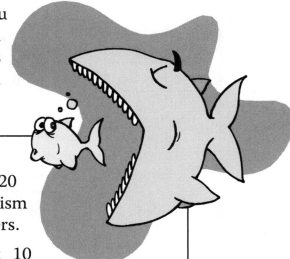

2 Points

❏ Make a food chain card game with at least 20 cards in which players need to categorize organism cards as producers, consumers, or decomposers.

❏ Make a food web flipbook with at least 10 producers, 5 consumers, and 2 decomposers.

5 Points

❏ Make a diorama that illustrates a food web found locally. Label each part of the diorama as living or nonliving.

❏ Write a letter to your local government office about the importance of maintaining local habitats. Include information about the food chains and how local habitat changes can impact food chains.

❏ Create an original song about food chains and how energy moves through them. Be prepared to teach your song to the class.

❏ Free choice—Prepare a proposal form and submit it to your teacher for approval.

8 Points

❏ Design an activity to present to the class that shows how energy flows through a food chain, as well as the effects of removing one part of the food chain.

❏ Make a PowerPoint presentation on food webs that includes at least one local food chain. Your presentation should also discuss factors that can change food webs.

Adaptations

Tic-Tac-Toe Menu

Objectives Covered Through This Menu and These Activities
- Students will identify adaptations that allow an organism to better survive in a habitat.
- Students will predict an organism's biome based on visible adaptations.
- Students will predict adaptations that would help an organism survive in a certain biome.

Materials Needed by Students for Completion
- Poster board or large white paper
- Shoebox (for diorama)
- Materials for student demonstration on adaptations
- Microsoft PowerPoint or other slideshow software
- Cube template

Special Notes on the Use of This Menu
This menu has two choices that really allow for reinforcement of adaptations. The quiz show is a fun way to have students review adaptations and biomes, and the student demonstration will also help review adaptations within a species.

Time Frame
- 2 weeks—Students are given the menu as the unit is started. As the teacher presents lessons throughout the week, he or she should refer back to the options associated with that content. The teacher will go over all of the options for that content and have students place checkmarks in the boxes that represent the activities they are most interested in completing. As teaching continues over the next 2 weeks, activities chosen and completed should make a column or a row. When students complete this pattern, they will have completed one activity from three different objectives.
- 1 week—At the start of the unit, the teacher chooses the three activities he or she feels are most valuable for the students. Stations can be set up in the classroom. These three activities are available for student choice throughout the week, as regular instruction takes place.
- 1–2 days—The teacher chooses an activity from the menu to use with the entire class.

Suggested Forms

- All purpose rubric
- Student-taught lesson rubric
- Proposal forms

Name:_____

Adaptations Menu

☐ *Develop a Demonstration* Choose one adaptation within a species (e.g., beaks or claws in birds) and create a demonstration for the class that shows how a species has different adaptations in order to survive in its specific environment.	☐ *Make a Poster* Research five different adaptations that animals have that help them survive in their environment. Make a poster with your information so it can be posted in the classroom.	☐ *Draw an Animal* Choose either the desert or forest biome. Create a make-believe animal that could survive there. Draw a picture of the animal and label its adaptations.
☐ *Draw a Mind Map* Draw a mind map that presents the different adaptations that animals have in the desert, tundra, and forest. In the mind map, include the animals, the adaptations, and the aspects of the environment that affect the adaptation.	☐ **Free Choice** (Fill out your proposal form before beginning the free choice!)	☐ *Create a Cube* Create an activity cube that has six different adaptations. Each side of the cube should include one adaptation, a description of the adaptation, and a drawing of an animal with that adaptation.
☐ *Design a Diorama* Design a diorama of a biome. In the diorama, include and label at least three living things with specific adaptations for that biome.	☐ *Prepare a Speech* Scientists can introduce a species into a new habitat to help control a local organism's out-of-control population. Scientists are thinking of introducing a variety of Barn Owls in Texas cities to try and control the cockroach problem. Could this be successful? Prepare a speech for your class that discusses your opinion.	☐ *Prepare a PowerPoint Presentation* Prepare a quiz show PowerPoint presentation that can be presented to the class. It should contain pictures of animals with adaptations and be presented to the class in such a way that classmates can guess what adaptations the animal has and what habitat or biome that animal calls home.

Check the boxes you plan to complete. They should form a tic-tac-toe across or down. All products are due by: _____.

Adaptations Cube

Complete the cube for adaptations. Use this pattern or create your own cube. Each side of the cube should include one adaptation, a description of the adaptation, and a drawing of an animal with that adaptation.

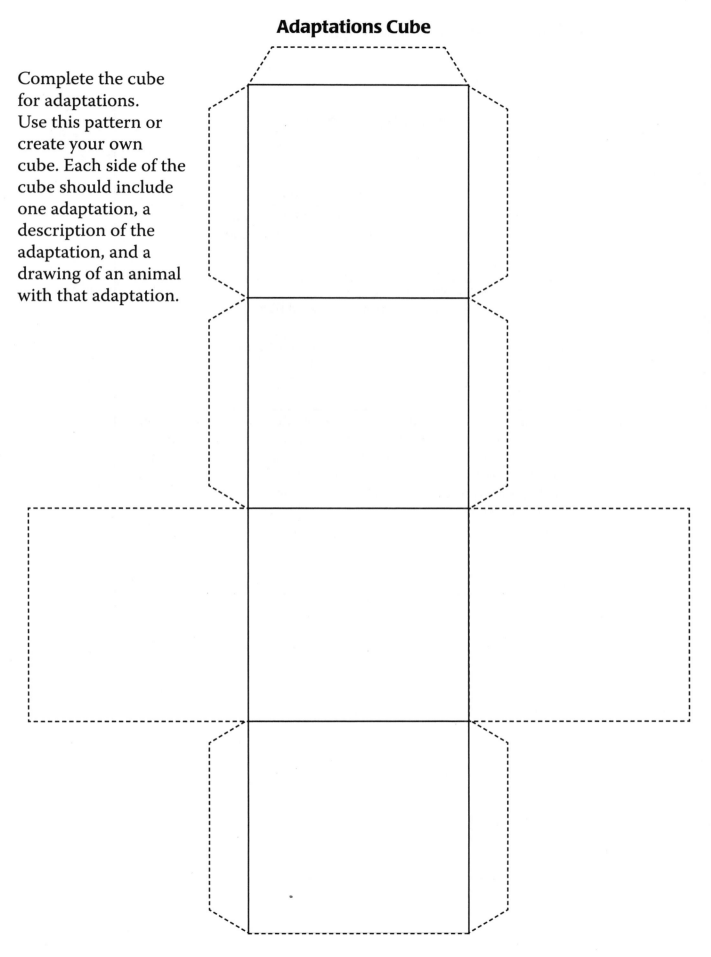

Cells and Their Organelles

2-5-8 Menu

Objectives Covered Through This Menu and These Activities

- Students will identify a cell's organelles and their locations.
- Students will tell how each organelle helps a cell function.

Materials Needed by Students for Completion

- Poster board or large white paper
- Graph paper or Internet access (for crossword puzzle)
- Cube template
- Materials for board games (e.g., folders, colored cards)
- Materials for constructing a model of a cell

Time Frame

- 1–2 weeks—Students are given the menu as the unit is started, and the teacher discusses all of the product options on the menu. As the different options are discussed, students will choose products that add to a total of 10 points. As the lessons progress through the week, the teacher and students refer back to the options associated with the content being taught.
- 1–2 days—The teacher chooses an activity from the menu to use with the entire class.

Suggested Forms

- All-purpose rubric
- Proposal form for point-based projects

Name:_____

Cells

Directions: Choose two activities from the menu below. The activities must total 10 points. Place a checkmark next to each box to show which activities you will complete. All activities must be completed by

_____.

---

2 Points

❏ Create a crossword puzzle on a cell's organelles and their functions.

❏ Make a cell cube. Each side will list an organelle, where it is located within the cell, its function, and a drawing or picture of the organelle.

---

5 Points

❏ Make a cell-themed board game.

❏ Create a three-dimensional model of a cell with all its organelles.

❏ Design a travel brochure for Cell City. Include information on all of the interesting sights a tourist should visit.

❏ Free choice—Prepare a proposal form and submit it to your teacher for approval.

---

8 Points

❏ It is your job to nominate one cell organelle for the cell "Wall of Fame." The nominee must be very deserving and important. Prepare a nomination speech for the organelle you think most deserves this honor.

❏ Create a three-dimensional model of a cell using objects for each organelle that represent the organelle's function (e.g., you could use a brain eraser for the nucleus). Label each object with the organelle's name.

Cells Cube

Complete the cube for cells. On each side, list an organelle, where it is located within the cell, its function, and a drawing or picture of the organelle. Use this pattern or create your own cube.

Human Body Systems

Baseball Menu

Objectives Covered Through This Menu and These Activities
- Students will investigate the circulatory, respiration, digestive, muscular, skeletal, and nervous systems.
- Students will identify the organs in different body systems.
- Students will explain how different organ systems impact the human body, as well as the importance of each organ within its system.

Materials Needed by Students for Completion
- Blank index cards (for trading cards)
- Materials for board games (e.g., folders, colored cards)
- Product cube template
- Ruler (for cartoons)
- Poster board or large piece of white paper
- Scrapbooking materials

Special Notes on the Use of This Menu
Most of the choices in this menu are not specific to a certain body system. Although this menu is set up with the expectations that students will complete a product that has information about each system, this menu could be used to reinforce just one system instead.

Time Frame
- 4 or more weeks—Students are given the menu as the unit starts with the expectation that by the end of the study of the human body, they will have completed a product about every system being discussed and earned 100 points in total. As each system is discussed, students are asked to choose one option for that system.
- 2–3 weeks—Students are given the menu as the system unit is started, and the guidelines and point expectations on the top of the menu are discussed. Students will place checkmarks in the boxes next to the activities they are most interested in completing. As instruction continues, activities are completed by the students and submitted for grading.
- 1 week—Students are given the menu with the expectation that they will complete 50 points on the body system currently being studied.

- 1–2 days—The teacher chooses an activity from an objective to use with the entire class during that lesson time.

Suggested Forms
- All-purpose rubric
- Proposal form for point-based projects

Human Body Systems Baseball

Look through the following choices and decide how you want to make your game add to 100 points. Singles are worth 10, Doubles are worth 30, Triples are worth 50, and Homeruns are worth 100. Choose any combination you want! Place a **checkmark** next to each choice you are going to complete. Make sure that your points equal 100!

These choices are not specific to one body system. When you decide on your choices, plan on including all of the following systems in your products. For example, if you complete a product that compares two systems, then you have completed two systems.

Digestive System	Circulatory System
Respiratory System	Nervous System
Skeletal System	Muscular System

Singles—10 Points Each

- ❑ Make a flipbook for two body systems. The flipbook must contain the organs in the system and the function of each.
- ❑ Create a set of trading cards for a body system of your choice.
- ❑ Create a worksheet about the body system of your choice and its functions.
- ❑ Create a human body system dictionary. It should include all of the systems and what purpose they serve in the human body.
- ❑ Design an acrostic by writing the name of the body system down the left side of the paper. Provide descriptions about the function of the system for each letter.
- ❑ Create a series of hand movements that shows how the circulatory system works. Share your movement with the class.
- ❑ Free choice—prepare a proposal form and submit it to your teacher for approval.

Doubles—30 Points Each

- ❑ Make a human body board game. It must contain information on all of the body systems.
- ❑ Create a body system flipbook. Use one flap for each body system. Draw the system and its organs, and describe how it helps the body to function.
- ❑ Design a product cube that analyzes the body system of your choice in depth.
- ❑ Build a model of your body system that shows all of the organs.
- ❑ Make an informational pamphlet on your body system and its importance to the body's function.
- ❑ Develop an advertisement for your body system. Include the functions of the system and its importance to the body.
- ❑ Free choice—prepare a proposal form and submit it to your teacher for approval.

Triples—50 Points Each

❑ Although all of the systems of the human body are interdependent, which system do you feel is the most important? Prepare a persuasive speech that explains and supports your point of view.

❑ Write a journal entry for a day in the life of a body system of your choice. Your day should begin when the body goes to sleep and continue for 24 hours.

❑ The Magic School Bus is taking a trip through your body system. Create a cartoon that documents the adventures.

❑ Prepare a You Be the Organ Presentation for your class in which you are an organ in the body system of your choice.

❑ Research diseases that cause damage to a body system of your choice. Make a poster about the common diseases and what can be done to prevent them.

Homerun—100 Points

❑ Create a human body family scrapbook. At least one page should be dedicated to each family member or body system, the system's organs, and their functions. It should also explain how each system is important to the body's total functions. Be creative in how you include the information.

I Chose:

_____ Singles (10 points each)

_____ Doubles (30 points each)

_____ Triples (50 points each)

_____ Homerun (100 points)

Human Body Cube

Complete the cube for the human body. Respond to the questions on each side to analyze your body system in depth. Use this pattern or create your own cube.

Describe your body system.

Compare and contrast your body system with another system.

List all of the organs in your body system and describe their function.

Discuss what would happen if your body system stopped working.

Name one disease that affects your body system. What are the symptoms and how does it affect your body system?

Describe how your body system works with the other systems in the body.

The Carbon and Nitrogen Cycle

2-5-8 Menu

Objectives Covered Through This Menu and These Activities
- Students will identify the parts of the carbon and nitrogen cycles.
- Students will understand the importance of the carbon and nitrogen cycles in their daily lives.
- Students will compare and contrast the carbon and nitrogen cycles.

Materials Needed by Students for Completion
- Index cards (for trading cards)
- Materials for board games (e.g., folders, colored cards)
- Various materials for student model of the nitrogen cycle

Special Notes on the Use of This Menu
Students have the option of making a two-sided flipbook. There are different ways for students to create this flip book. The easiest way would have students create two flipbooks and glue them back to back.

Time Frame
- 1–2 weeks—Students are given the menu as the unit is started, and the teacher discusses all of the product options on the menu. As the different options are discussed, students will choose products that add to a total of 10 points. As the lessons progress through the week, the teacher and students refer back to the options associated with the content being taught.
- 1–2 days—The teacher chooses an activity from the menu to use with the entire class.

Suggested Forms
- All-purpose rubric

Name:_____

The Carbon and Nitrogen Cycles

Directions: Choose two activities from the menu below. The activities must total 10 points. Place a checkmark next to each box to show which activities you will complete. All activities must be completed by

_____.

2 Points

❏ Make a two-sided flipbook on the carbon and nitrogen cycles. One side should have the carbon cycle and its components, and the other side should have the nitrogen cycle and its components.

❏ Make two teams of trading cards: the carbon cycle team and the nitrogen cycle team. Include the information about the parts of the cycle, as well as their importance on each card.

5 Points

❏ Make a board game that features either the carbon cycle or the nitrogen cycle as your theme.

❏ Draw a Venn diagram that compares and contrasts the carbon and nitrogen cycles.

❏ Design an advertisement for the carbon cycle. Include how the cycle works and its importance to our lives.

❏ Create a model of the nitrogen cycle. Label each part.

8 Points

❏ Write a story from the viewpoint of a local tree. Explain the part it plays in the carbon cycle and how the carbon cycle might be affected if something happened to the tree or its fellow trees.

❏ Examine the nitrogen cycle. Which part of the cycle do you think is most important? Create a persuasive speech for the class that shares why you feel this way.

The Water Cycle

2-5-8 Menu

Objectives Covered Through This Menu and These Activities

- Students will identify the steps of the water cycle.
- Students will understand what occurs as water travels through the water cycle.
- Students will demonstrate the water cycle.
- Students will understand the importance of the water cycle on our daily lives.

Materials Needed by Students for Completion

- Blank index cards (for concentration cards)
- Graph paper or Internet access (for crossword puzzle)
- Various lab materials for water cycle experiment

Time Frame

- 1–2 weeks—Students are given the menu as the unit is started, and the teacher discusses all of the product options on the menu. As the different options are discussed, students will choose products that add to a total of 10 points. As the lessons progress through the week, the teacher and students refer back to the options associated with the content being taught.
- 1–2 days—The teacher chooses an activity from the menu to use with the entire class.

Suggested Forms

- Lab report rubric
- All-purpose rubric
- Student-taught lesson rubric

The Water Cycle

Directions: Choose two activities from the menu below. The activities must total 10 points. Place a checkmark next to each box to show which activities you will complete. All activities must be completed by

_____.

---

2 Points

❑ Create a water cycle flipbook. The outside will show the stages of the water cycle. Record detailed information about each stage inside each flap.

❑ Make a concentration card set for the key ideas and concepts of the water cycle.

---

5 Points

❑ There is a new book about the water cycle being published. They have asked you to design a book cover for it. Be sure and include a catchy title!

❑ Create a song to help you remember the steps of the water cycle, as well as what happens during each stage. Teach your song to the class.

❑ Create a board game with a water cycle theme.

❑ Make a crossword puzzle using key terms from the water cycle. Have a classmate complete your puzzle.

---

8 Points

❑ Design a scientific experiment that demonstrates the water cycle. Present the experiment to your class. Turn in your lab report before demonstrating the experiment.

❑ Teach a lesson to the class on the water cycle and its importance in our daily lives.

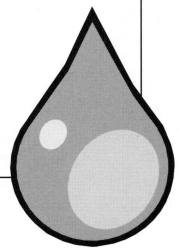

Plant and Animal Life Cycles

2-5-8 Menu

Objectives Covered Through This Menu and These Activities
- Students will identify the parts of the plant and animal life cycles.
- Students will compare and contrast plant and animal life cycles.

Materials Needed by Students for Completion
- Coat hangers (for mobile)
- Index cards (for mobile)
- String (for mobile)
- Large white paper (for mural)
- Scrapbooking materials

Time Frame
- 1–2 weeks—Students are given the menu as the unit is started, and the teacher discusses all of the product options on the menu. As the different options are discussed, students will choose products that add to a total of 10 points. As the lessons progress through the week, the teacher and students refer back to the options associated with the content being taught.
- 1–2 days—The teacher chooses an activity from the menu to use with the entire class.

Suggested Forms
- All-purpose rubric
- Proposal form for point-based projects

Life Cycles of Plants and Animals

Directions: Choose two activities from the menu below. The activities must total 10 points. Place a checkmark next to each box to show which activities you will complete. All activities must be completed by _____.

---

2 Points

❐ Draw the life cycle of a plant and an animal of your choice. Label the stages.

❐ Make a mobile that shows the life cycle of a specific plant or animal. Design it so the order of the cycle is clear.

---

5 Points

❐ Compare and contrast the life cycles of a plant and an animal using a Venn diagram.

❐ Create a mural that shows how an organism changes as it goes through its life cycle.

❐ Make a scrapbook (family album) for a seed or an egg. Your scrapbook needs to include all of the family members.

❐ Free choice—prepare a proposal form and submit it to your teacher for approval.

---

8 Points

❐ Write a book from the viewpoint of a seed or an egg. Tell how it feels as you change and grow.

❐ Create an interview for a caterpillar about its upcoming life changes. What will happen? Is the caterpillar excited? Conduct the make-believe interview on paper and share the caterpillar's answers with your classmates.

CHAPTER 7

Earth Science

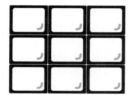

Our Oceans

Game Show Menu

Objectives Covered Through This Menu and These Activities

- Students will identify various life forms found in the ocean.
- Students will locate large bodies of salt water on the earth's surface.
- Students will indicate characteristics of an ocean.
- Students will explain what causes tides.
- Students will understand how oceans help in their daily lives.

Materials Needed by Students for Completion

- Coat hangers (for mobile)
- Index cards (for mobile)
- String (for mobile)
- Shoe boxes (for diorama)
- Product cube template
- Poster board or large white paper

Time Frame

- 2–3 weeks—Students are given the menu as the unit is started and the guidelines and point expectations on the menu are discussed. As lessons are taught throughout the unit, students and the teacher can refer back to the options associated with that topic. The teacher will go over all of the options for the topic being covered and have students place checkmarks in the boxes next to the activities they are most interested in completing. As teaching continues throughout the 2–3 weeks, the activities are discussed, chosen, and submitted for grading.
- 1 week—At the beginning of the unit, the teacher chooses an activity from each area that he or she feels would be most valuable for the students. Stations can be set up in the classroom. These activities are available for student choice throughout the week, as regular instruction takes place.
- 1–2 days—The teacher chooses an activity from an objective to use with the entire class during that lesson time.

Suggested Forms

- All-purpose rubric

Guidelines for Our Oceans Game Show Menu

- You must choose at least one activity from each topic area.
- You may not do more than two activities in any one topic area for credit. (You are, of course, welcome to do more than two for your own investigation.)
- Grading will be ongoing, so turn in products as you complete them.
- All free-choice proposals must be turned in and approved *prior* to working on that free choice.
- You must earn 100 points for a 100%. You may earn extra credit up to _____ points.
- You must show your teacher your plan for completion by: _____.

Our Oceans

Ocean Animals	Locations on Earth	Characteristics	Tides	Oceans and Our Lives	Points for Each Level
☐ Create a mobile of life forms found in the ocean. (10 pts.)	☐ Draw a map that features the large bodies of water on the earth. (15 pts.)	☐ Develop a windowpane that shows six characteristics of an ocean. (10 pts.)	☐ Create a poster that explains why tides occur and how they change daily. (10 pts.)	☐ Produce a poster that shows how oceans help us in our lives. (10 pts.)	10–15 points
☐ Design a diorama that shows the areas of the ocean and its floor. Include at least one living thing in each area of the diorama. (25 pts.)	☐ Make a project cube for six large bodies of water. Include their location, and characteristics, and the life forms found in each. (20 pts.)	☐ Create a Venn diagram to compare and contrast the Atlantic and Pacific Oceans. (20 pts.)	☐ Record high and low tides at a beach of your choice for one week. Present the information and draw conclusions about the patterns you observe. (25 pts.)	☐ Create an advertisement for an ocean item (other than a food item) that is useful to humans. (25 pts.)	20–25 points
☐ There are many living things in the ocean that have not yet been discovered. Write a story that tells of a new life form you have discovered. Include a drawing of it. (30 pts.)	☐ Create an original song or rap about the major bodies of water and their locations. (30 pts.)	☐ Write a poem about the ocean and what makes it special to you. (30 pts.)	☐ Write a journal entry from the viewpoint of a fiddler crab. Explain what happens to you as the tides occur throughout the day. (30 pts.)	☐ There are many rules for use of our oceans to promote preservation. Write a letter to your congressperson discussing whether or not you feel oceans should be preserved. (30 pts.)	30 points
Free Choice (prior approval) (25–50 pts.)	**Free Choice** (prior approval) (25–50 pts.)	**Free Choice** (prior approval) (25–50 pts.)	**Free Choice** (prior approval) (25–50 pts.)	**Free Choice** (prior approval) (25–50 pts.)	25–50 points
Total:	**Total:**	**Total:**	**Total:**	**Total:**	**Total Grade:**

Oceans Cube

Complete the cube for the ocean. Use the cube to represent six large bodies of water. On each side, include each one's location, characteristics, and life forms. Use this pattern or create your own cube.

Our Soil

Tic-Tac-Toe Menu

Objectives Covered Through This Menu and These Activities
- Students will describe how soil is created.
- Students will identity different types of soil.
- Students will test soil's ability to retain water.
- Students will examine soil for its color and texture.
- Students will debate the best uses for different soil types.

Materials Needed by Students for Completion
- Poster board or large white paper
- Heavy weight paper (for instruction card)
- Various lab materials for water retention experiment
- Three different types of soil
- Colored paper (for birthday card)
- Hand lens

Special Notes on the Use of This Menu
This menu has two options in which students will share information with their classmates. For the first, students will share their findings on different soils' ability to retain water. The other will share which type of soil is best for farmers. Both of these presentations should not exceed 5 minutes each.

Time Frame
- 2 weeks—Students are given the menu as the unit is started. As the teacher presents lessons throughout the week, he or she should refer back to the options associated with that content. The teacher will go over all of the options for that content and have students place checkmarks in the boxes that represent the activities they are most interested in completing. As teaching continues over the next 2 weeks, activities chosen and completed should make a column or a row. When students complete this pattern, they will have completed one activity from three different objectives.
- 1 week—At the start of the unit, the teacher chooses the three activities he or she feels are most valuable for the students. Stations can be set up in the classroom. These three activities are available for student choice throughout the week, as regular instruction takes place.

- 1–2 days—The teacher chooses an activity from the menu to use with the entire class.

Suggested Forms

- Lab report rubric
- All-purpose rubric
- Proposal forms

Our Soil

☐ *Present a Poster* Research how soil is naturally created. Make a poster that demonstrates the steps. Include a picture for each step.	☐ *Develop an Instruction Card* Soils are different from one another. Develop an instruction card that helps identify one type of soil from another. Use words, drawings, and pictures to help in the identification.	☐ *Prepare a Presentation* Not all soils can be used for all purposes. Prepare a presentation for the class that shows which of the test soils would be best for farmers to use. Be sure that you support your recommendation with experimental facts.
☐ *Design an Experiment* Design an experiment to test a soil's capacity to retain water. Conduct the experiment and share the results with your class. Submit a lab report with your findings.	☐ **Free Choice** (Fill out your proposal form before beginning the free choice!)	☐ *Design a Birthday Card* Soil can take a long time to create. Design a birthday card for 100-year-old soil. Include a personal message about its life experiences in those 100 years.
☐ *Create an Advertisement* Fertile soil has its obvious advantages and uses, but what about sandy soil? Create an advertisement for sandy soil. Focus on its benefits and uses.	☐ *Complete a Collection* Collect at least five different samples of soil. Label where each was collected. Design a way to display your samples, with information on each soil's color, their textures, and their ability to retain water.	☐ *Record Data Through Drawing* Using a hand lens, examine three different types of soil. Using color, draw what you see.

Check the boxes you plan to complete. They should form a tic-tac-toe across or down. All products are due by: _____.

The Rock Cycle

2-5-8 Menu

Objectives Covered Through This Menu and These Activities

- Students will identify the different steps of the rock cycle.
- Students will explain how a rock changes as it goes through the rock cycle.

Materials Needed by Students for Completion

- Graph paper or Internet access (for crossword puzzle)
- Materials for board games (e.g., folders, colored cards)
- Scrapbooking materials

Time Frame

- 1–2 weeks—Students are given the menu as the unit is started, and the teacher discusses all of the product options on the menu. As the different options are discussed, students will choose products that add to a total of 10 points. As the lessons progress through the week, the teacher and students refer back to the options associated with the content being taught.
- 1–2 days—The teacher chooses an activity from the menu to use with the entire class.

Suggested Forms

- All-purpose rubric
- Student-taught lesson rubric

Name:_____

The Rock Cycle

Directions: Choose two activities from the menu below. The activities must total 10 points. Place a checkmark next to each box to show which activities you will complete. All activities must be completed by _____.

2 Points

❑ Create a flipbook on the rock cycle. The cover should have a drawing of the rock cycle, and each flap should include details about the different processes and rock types of the rock cycle.

❑ Make a crossword puzzle about the rock cycle with an answer key. Have a classmate complete the puzzle.

5 Points

❑ Write a journal entry for a rock's journey through the rock cycle.

❑ Create a thematic board game based on the steps and type of rocks in the rock cycle.

❑ Create a scrapbook for the life of a rock as it went through the rock cycle. Be creative when describing its adventures.

❑ Prepare a news report about an igneous rock's change into sedimentary rock. Consider the kinds of questions a reporter would ask. Answer the questions about "who" the rock is, what has happened, and where and how it all took place. Have fun!

8 Points

❑ Create an original song or rap to help learn the steps of the rock cycle. Teach your song to the class.

❑ Write a fictional play that shows the drama of the changes in the rock cycle. Be creative!

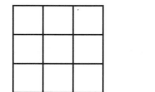

Earth Processes

Tic-Tac-Toe Menu

Objectives Covered Through This Menu and These Activities

- Students will define the processes of weathering, erosion, and deposition.
- Students will identify various landforms caused by earth processes.
- Students will discuss ways to prevent erosion.
- Students will identify agents of erosion.

Materials Needed by Students for Completion

- Poster board or large white paper
- Various lab materials for erosion demonstration

Special Notes on the Use of This Menu

Students have the option to present a demonstration on erosion. This demonstration should not take longer than 10 minutes and can be used to reinforce the lessons being taught on erosion. Have the students present their demonstration as a warm-up to the daily lesson or as reinforcement at the end of the lesson.

Time Frame

- 2 weeks—Students are given the menu as the unit is started. As the teacher presents lessons throughout the week, he or she should refer back to the options associated with that content. The teacher will go over all of the options for that content and have students place checkmarks in the boxes that represent the activities they are most interested in completing. As teaching continues over the next 2 weeks, activities chosen and completed should make a column or a row. When students complete this pattern, they will have completed one activity from three different objectives.
- 1 week—At the start of the unit, the teacher chooses the three activities he or she feels are most valuable for the students. Stations can be set up in the classroom. These three activities are available for student choice throughout the week, as regular instruction takes place.
- 1–2 days—The teacher chooses an activity from the menu to use with the entire class.

Suggested Forms
- Lab report rubric
- All-purpose rubric
- Proposal forms

Name:_____

Earth Processes

☐ *Make a Windowpane* There are many land features caused by deposition. Make a windowpane of these features and depict where they usually form.	☐ *Design a Demonstration* Erosion takes place every day, in many places. Design a demonstration that shows how erosion takes place.	☐ *Develop a Slogan* People often confuse weathering with erosion. Develop a slogan or catchy phrase to help people remember the difference.
☐ *Prepare a Speech* In your opinion, is weathering a beneficial earth process? Give concrete examples to support your viewpoint.	☐ *Free Choice* (Fill out your proposal form before beginning the free choice!)	☐ *Create a Flipbook* Create a flipbook that shows the various agents of erosion. Describe each one and where it takes place.
☐ *Create an Advertisement* Create an advertisement for a plan that could help prevent erosion. Include pictures of the plan, as well as a description of how the plan will work.	☐ *Make a Poster* Make a poster that shows weathering and where it takes place.	☐ *Write a Story* You are a rock. Write a story describing your adventure of being eroded, weathered, and finally deposited.

Check the boxes you plan to complete. They should form a tic-tac-toe across or down. All products are due by: _____.

Fossils and Fossil Records

2-5-8 Menu

Objectives Covered Through This Menu and These Activities

- Students will identify trace, mold, and cast fossils.
- Students will make their own fossils.
- Students will apply the law of superposition.
- Students will investigate how scientists determine the age of a fossil.

Materials Needed by Students for Completion

- Poster board or large white paper
- Blank index cards (for concentration game)
- Box (for archeological dig)
- Microsoft PowerPoint or other slideshow software
- Video camera (for television show)

Time Frame

- 1–2 weeks—Students are given the menu as the unit is started, and the teacher discusses all of the product options on the menu. As the different options are discussed, students will choose products that add to a total of 10 points. As the lessons progress through the week, the teacher and students refer back to the options associated with the content being taught.
- 1–2 days—The teacher chooses an activity from the menu to use with the entire class.

Suggested Forms

- All-purpose rubric

Name:_____

Fossils and Fossil Records

Directions: Choose two activities from the menu below. The activities must total 10 points. Place a checkmark next to each box to show which activities you will complete. All activities must be completed by

_____.

---

2 Points

❏ Make a three-box windowpane for trace, mold, and cast fossils.

❏ Create a concentration game for different examples of each type of fossil.

---

5 Points

❏ Archeologists can determine a fossil's relative age by comparing its location within rock layers. This is called the law of superposition. Research this law and design an educational poster to explain what you've learned.

❏ Create an archeological dig box that shows how archeologists process an area for artifacts and fossils.

❏ Research how scientists determine the age of a fossil. Create a PowerPoint presentation to explain how they date fossils with at least one example.

❏ Free choice—Prepare a proposal form and submit it to your teacher for approval.

---

8 Points

❏ While walking on the beach, you discover a trilobite fossil. Write a story or play that tells how the trilobite went from a living thing to washing up at your feet on the beach.

❏ Create an educational television show about fossils. It must be informational, creative, fun, and interesting!

Our Earth's Resources

List Menu

Objectives Covered Through This Menu and These Activities
- Students will identify resources as renewable, nonrenewable, or inexhaustible.
- Students will encourage conservation of our natural resources.
- Students will predict the implications of the depletion of certain nonrenewable resources.

Materials Needed by Students for Completion
- Magazines (for collage)
- Graph paper or Internet access (for crossword puzzle)
- Poster board or large white paper
- Microsoft PowerPoint or other slideshow software
- Video camera (optional for public service announcement)

Special Notes on the Use of This Menu
Students can choose to create a PowerPoint presentation in which classmates can guess what types of resources are shown. This can be used as a warm-up for a classroom lesson, or it would be a wonderful review before an assessment.

Time Frame
- 1–2 weeks—Students are given the menu as the unit is started and the guidelines and point expectations are discussed. Because this menu covers one topic in depth, the teacher will go over all of the options on the menu and have students place checkmarks in the boxes next to the activities they are most interested in completing. Once the students have placed check marks next to the activities they are interested in, teachers will set aside a few moments to sign the agreement at the bottom of the page with each student. As instruction continues, activities are completed by students and submitted for grading.
- 1–2 days—The teacher chooses an activity from an objective to use with the entire class during that lesson time.

Suggested Forms
- All purpose rubric

Name:_____

Our Earth's Resources Challenge
Renewable, Nonrenewable, and Inexhaustible Resources

Guidelines:
1. You may complete as many of the activities listed within the time period.
2. You may choose any combination of activities.
3. Your goal is 100 points. You may earn up to _____ points extra credit.
4. You may be as creative as you like within the guidelines listed below.
5. You must show your plan to your teacher by _____.
6. Activities may be turned in at any time during the working time period. They will be graded and recorded on this sheet as you continue to work, so keep it safe!

Plan to Do	Activity to Complete	Point Value	Date Completed	Points Earned
	Create a collage with pictures of a variety of resources found on earth. Label each resource as renewable, nonrenewable, or inexhaustible.	30		
	Design a crossword puzzle with at least 20 significant vocabulary words for resources.	30		
	Complete another student's crossword puzzle.	15		
	Design a bumper sticker to encourage conservation of a nonrenewable resource.	35		
	Choose a nonrenewable resource. Write a story predicting how our lives will change when this resource runs out.	40		
	Make an acrostic for one of these words: renewable, nonrenewable, or inexhaustible. Use examples or properties for the letter of the word you have chosen.	25		
	Make an educational poster on these three types of resources.	20		
	Create a PowerPoint quiz game where participants have to guess whether a resource is renewable, nonrenewable, or inexhaustible.	30		
	Draw a mind map of different resources with examples.	20		
	A friend has told you it is impossible to find a resource that is inexhaustible. Prepare a response to his or her statement.	40		
	Develop a public service announcement for the conservation of our natural resources.	35		
	Choose a nonrenewable resource that you feel is important to conserve. Interview a local community member who works with this resource. What conservation efforts are being taken?	30		
	Free choice: Must be outlined on a proposal form and approved before beginning work.			
	Total number of points you are planning to earn.		**Total points earned:**	

I am planning to complete _____ activities that could earn up to a total of _____ points.

Teacher's initials _____ Student's signature _____

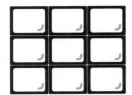

Our Weather

Game Show Menu

Objectives Covered Through This Menu and These Activities

- Students will identify the different types of clouds.
- Students will categorize clouds and the weather associated with each type.
- Students will interpret weather maps.
- Students will interpret weather map symbols.
- Students will create their own weather maps.
- Students will identify dangerous weather phenomena and its causes.
- Students will describe weather instruments and their uses including an anemometer, hygrometer, barometer, and rain gauge.

Materials Needed by Students for Completion

- Camera (for cloud photo)
- Newspaper (for weather maps)
- Access to Internet and television weather reports
- Poster board or large white paper
- Microsoft PowerPoint or other slideshow software
- Socks (for puppets)
- Paper bags (for puppets)
- Various materials for student-created weather instrument

Special Notes on the Use of This Menu

This menu has at least four opportunities for students to present information to the class. In an ideal situation, the menu is expected to take at least 3 weeks, so there should be time to work the presentations easily into the daily instruction as topics are covered.

Time Frame

- 2–3 weeks—Students are given the menu as the unit is started and the guidelines and point expectations on the menu are discussed. As lessons are taught throughout the unit, students and the teacher can refer back to the options associated with that topic. The teacher will go over all of the options for the topic being covered and have students place checkmarks in the boxes next to the activities they are most interested in completing. As teaching continues throughout the

2–3 weeks, the activities are discussed, chosen, and submitted for grading.

- 1 week—At the beginning of the unit, the teacher chooses an activity from each area that he or she feels would be most valuable for the students. Stations can be set up in the classroom. These activities are available for student choice throughout the week, as regular instruction takes place.
- 1–2 days—The teacher chooses an activity from an objective to use with the entire class during that lesson time.

Suggested Forms

- All-purpose rubric

Guidelines for Our Weather Game Show Menu

- You must choose at least one activity from each topic area.
- You may not do more than two activities in any one topic area for credit. (You are, of course, welcome to do more than two for your own investigation.)
- Grading will be ongoing, so turn in products as you complete them.
- All free-choice proposals must be turned in and approved *prior* to working on that free choice.
- You must earn 110 points for a 100%. You may earn extra credit up to _____ points.
- You must show your teacher your plan for completion by: _____.

Our Weather

Points for Each Level	Clouds	Weather Maps	Weather Phenomena	Weather Symbols	Weather Instruments
10–15 points	☐ Using a camera, take photos of at least five different types of clouds. Label each type of cloud and record what type of weather is associated with that cloud. (15 pts.)	☐ Choose a national weather map from the newspaper or an Internet site. Create a worksheet that asks weather-based questions about the map and have another student answer the worksheet. (15 pts.)	☐ Make a poster of dangerous weather-related phenomena. Include pictures of each and a brief explanation of its cause. (10 pts.)	☐ Make a weather map key. Show the common symbols used on weather maps and their meanings. (10 pts.)	☐ Find a picture of an anemometer, a hygrometer, a barometer, a thermometer, and a rain gauge. Label each picture and describe what each measures. (15 pts.)
20–25 points	☐ Make an informational brochure about the different types of clouds. Include pictures of each type of cloud, how to identify it, and the weather associated with it. (25 pts.)	☐ Cut out the national weather map from the newspaper for one week. Write a summary of each map including large weather patterns. (20 pts.)	☐ Create an advertisement for a hurricane- or tornado-proof building. Include how it is designed and its construction materials. (25 pts.)	☐ Research the origins of the weather symbols used on maps. Create a PowerPoint presentation on how and why these symbols were created. (20 pts.)	☐ Create a weather instrument puppet. Have the puppet explain how it works and how it helps meteorologists with the weather. (25 pts.)
30 points	☐ Create an original song to help you remember the types of clouds and the weather associated with each. Teach your song to your classmates. (30 pts.)	☐ Are all weather maps the same? Compare maps presented in the newspaper, on at least two different television channels, and the Internet. Create a book that describes each type of map. Choose which one you like best and explain why this was the best in your opinion. (30 pts.)	☐ What do you think is the worst weather phenomena in your area? Design a public service announcement educating the public about the dangers and how to cope with the weather occurrence. (30 pts.)	☐ Design a realistic weather map for your local area. Present your weather report to your class. (30 pts.)	☐ Build your own working weather instrument. Test it and record the data you collect. Include instructions on how you constructed the instrument. (30 pts.)
25–50 points	**Free Choice** (prior approval) (25–50 pts.)	**Free Choice** (prior approval) (25–50 pts.)	**Free Choice** (prior approval) (25–50 pts.)	**Free Choice** (prior approval) (25–50 pts.)	**Free Choice** (prior approval) (25–50 pts.)
Total Grade:	Total:	Total:	Total:	Total:	Total:

Planetary Baseball Menu

Objectives Covered Through This Menu and These Activities

- Students will put in order the planets in our solar system.
- Students will recognize the planets and their respective scales.
- Students will state the general characteristics of each planet.
- Students will investigate how the planets got their names.
- Students will research the formation of the asteroid belt.
- Students will compare the characteristics of the inner plants with the outer planets.

Materials Needed by Students for Completion

- Coat hangers (for mobile)
- Index cards (for mobile
- String (for mobile)
- Blank index cards (for trading cards and concentration game)
- Various materials for the planet model
- Poster board or large white paper
- Scrapbooking materials
- Microsoft PowerPoint or other slideshow software

Special Notes on the Use of This Menu

This menu has one activity that students can choose to teach their classmates the order and relative sizes of the planets. This activity can be used as a warm-up for a lesson on a particular planet or as a review before the test.

Time Frame

- 1–2 weeks—Students are given the menu as the unit is started and the guidelines and point expectations on the top of the menu are discussed. Usually, students are expected to complete 100 points. Because this menu covers one topic in depth, the teacher will go over all of the options for the topic being covered and have students place checkmarks in the boxes next to the activities they are most interested in completing. As instruction continues, the activities are completed by students and submitted for grading.
- 1–2 days—The teacher chooses an activity from an objective to use with the entire class during the lesson time.

Suggested Forms

- All-purpose rubric
- Student-taught lesson rubric

Name:_____

Planetary Baseball

Look through the following choices and decide how you want to make your game add to **100 points**. Singles are worth 10, Doubles are worth 30, Triples are worth 50, and Homeruns are worth 100. Choose any combination you want! Place a **checkmark** next to each choice you are going to complete. Make sure that your points equal 100!

Singles—10 Points Each

- ❑ On a long piece of butcher paper, draw the planets according to scale and color them as accurately as possible.
- ❑ Create a planet mobile with at least two facts about each planet.
- ❑ Create a set of trading cards for the planets of our solar system.
- ❑ Make a flipbook for the solar system. On the front, draw the planets in order; on the inside flaps, record information about each planet.
- ❑ Make a cross-sectional model of one of the planets in the solar system. Be as realistic as possible concerning its color and size.
- ❑ Create a concentration game to help other students learn the planets and their characteristics.
- ❑ Develop a worksheet for younger students to complete about the planets and their characteristics.

Doubles—30 Points Each

- ❑ Create an original song to help remember the names of the planets in order and at least three details about each.
- ❑ Create a travel brochure highlighting a planet of your choice.
- ❑ Research the history describing how the planets were named. Make an instructional poster that explains how each planet received its name.
- ❑ Venus is often called Earth's twin. Using a Venn diagram, compare and contrast Earth and Venus.
- ❑ Research the asteroid belt. Prepare a report that describes the asteroid belt and discusses how scientists think it came to exist in its present location.
- ❑ Create a solar system scrapbook with at least one page dedicated to each planet.
- ❑ Your friend the astronomer has just finished a book on the outer planets called "It's All Gas!" Design a book cover for your friend's book.

Triples—50 Points Each

❑ Create an activity for putting the planets in order and calculating their relative sizes. Be prepared to share your activity with your classmates.

❑ Develop a PowerPoint quiz show with little known facts about our planets.

❑ Think about which planet you think has the most interesting features. Write a poem about that planet and include references to some of its amazing features.

❑ Write an original myth to explain why Jupiter has a red spot.

❑ Choose one of the planets you find fascinating. Think about what kind of alien could survive on that planet. Include a written description of this alien, as well as a drawing that shows the alien's adaptations.

Homerun—100 Points Each

❑ Design a cruise brochure (booklet) and itinerary for an interplanetary cruise company. This company will be selling space cruises from the Earth to Mercury, and then out to Pluto and eventually returning to Earth. Of course, this cruise will be stopping at all planets and points of interest in between. Your booklet should include a realistic itinerary with travel times and the various planets or ports the cruise will visit as it travels. Each port should have its own page of information including side trips planned to points of interest on that planet. Finally, include a description of the ship and a pricing page based on the cabin chosen by the tourist.

I Chose:

_____ Singles (10 points each)

_____ Doubles (30 points each)

_____ Triples (50 points each)

_____ Homerun (100 points)

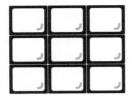

Space

Game Show Menu

Objectives Covered Through This Menu and These Activities

- Students will identify parts of the sun and their location.
- Students will identify characteristics of the inner planets.
- Students will identify characteristics of the outer planets.
- Students will discuss the properties of comets, meteorites, and asteroids.
- Students will identify items needed for space travel.
- Students will research the history of constellations and how they received their name.
- Students will investigate scientists related to space.

Materials Needed by Students for Completion

- Coat hangers (for mobile)
- Index cards (for mobile)
- String (for mobile)
- Project cube template
- Materials for board games (e.g., folders, colored cards)
- Blank cards (for match game)
- Show boxes (for diorama)

Time Frame

- 2–3 weeks—Students are given the menu as the unit is started and the guidelines and point expectations on the menu are discussed. As lessons are taught throughout the unit, students and the teacher can refer back to the options associated with that topic. The teacher will go over all of the options for the topic being covered and have students place checkmarks in the boxes next to the activities they are most interested in completing. As teaching continues throughout the 2–3 weeks, the activities are discussed, chosen, and submitted for grading.
- 1 week—At the beginning of the unit, the teacher chooses an activity from each area that he or she feels would be most valuable for the students. Stations can be set up in the classroom. These activities are available for student choice throughout the week, as regular instruction takes place.

- 1–2 days—The teacher chooses an activity from an objective to use with the entire class during that lesson time.

Suggested Forms
- All-purpose rubric

Guidelines for Space Game Show Menu

- You must choose at least one activity from each topic area.
- You may not do more than two activities in any one topic area for credit. (You are, of course, welcome to do more than two for your own investigation.)
- Grading will be ongoing, so turn in products as you complete them.
- All free-choice proposals must be turned in and approved *prior* to working on that free choice.
- You must earn 150 points for a 100%. You may earn extra credit up to _____ points.
- You must show your teacher your plan for completion by: _____.

Space

Points for Each Level	The Sun	The Inner Planets	The Outer Planets	Comets, Meteors, and Asteroids	Space Travel	Stars and Constellations	Space Scientists
10–15 points	☐ Create a mobile of the sun. Include the sun, its parts and their functions, and a drawing of the sun and its parts. (10 pts.)	☐ Make a windowpane for the inner planets. Include a drawing and at least five characteristics of each planet. (10 pts.)	☐ Make a flipbook on the outer planets. Include drawings and at least five characteristics for each. (10 pts.)	☐ Create a card match game for comets, meteors, and asteroids Include characteristics of each, a picture, and its location in the solar system. (10 pts.)	☐ Draw a rocket and record at least six items you would need to travel in space. (10 pts.)	☐ Create a book cover for a book about the history of constellations and how they got their names. Be sure to title the book. (15 pts.)	☐ List 15 scientists related to the study of space with a brief explanation as to what their contributions have been to the field. (15 pts.)
20–25 points	☐ Create a project cube that describes how the sun affects our daily lives in six unexpected ways. Each side should also include a picture. (20 pts.)	☐ Create a song or rap about the inner planets, and include characteristics about each planet. (25 pts.)	☐ Create an outer planet board game with pieces, cards, and a game board. Include the rules for playing. (25 pts.)	☐ Create a diorama of the solar system with comets, meteors, and asteroids. They must be in the proper location and scaled to size. (20 pts.)	☐ Create an advertisement for a piece of equipment necessary for space travel. (25 pts.)	☐ Create a Venn diagram that compares and contrasts our sun to a red giant. (20 pts.)	☐ Research and create a product on a scientist related to the study of space or space travel. (25 pts.)
30 points	☐ Choose the most important part of the sun in your opinion and write a story about what would happen if it ceased to exist. (30 pts.)	☐ The president has decided to make a space colony on one of the inner planets. Create an argument for the planet they should choose and why. (30 pts.)	☐ Create a drawing or model of an alien that could survive on one of the outer planets. Label all adaptations and how they help with survival. (30 pts.)	☐ There have been many movies about asteroids, comets, or meteors destroying Earth. View one of these movies and evaluate it for scientific truth. (30 pts.)	☐ You are a space equipment salesperson. Design a way to persuade NASA to buy your most inventive yet necessary piece of equipment. (30 pts.)	☐ Choose your favorite constellation in the night sky. Create your own myth that could explain how it got its name and arrangement. (30 pts.)	☐ Create a presentation for the class on a famous space scientist and pretend you are the scientist. (30 pts.)
25–50 points	Free Choice (prior approval) (25–50 pts.)	Free Choice (prior approval) (25–50 pts.)	Free Choice (prior approval) (25–50 pts.)	Free Choice (prior approval) (25–50 pts.)	Free Choice (prior approval) (25–50 pts.)	Free Choice (prior approval) (25–50 pts.)	Free Choice (prior approval) (25–50 pts.)
Total Grade:	Total:	Total:	Total:	Total:	Total:	Total:	Total:

Sun Cube

Complete a cube for your study of the sun. Each side of the cube should describe one way the sun affects our daily lives in unexpected ways. Include a picture or drawing on each side. Use this pattern or create your own cube.

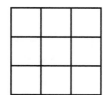

The Sun

Tic-Tac-Toe Menu

Objectives Covered Through This Menu and These Activities

- Students will name the parts of the sun.
- Students will predict what may happen when the sun begins to cool.
- Students will share how the sun impacts our daily lives.

Materials Needed by Students for Completion

- Coat hangers (for mobile)
- Index cards (for mobile)
- String (for mobile)
- Ruler (for comic strip)
- Materials for model of the sun (e.g., paint, Styrofoam balls)

Time Frame

- 2 weeks—Students are given the menu as the unit is started. As the teacher presents lessons throughout the week, he or she should refer back to the options associated with that content. The teacher will go over all of the options for that content and have students place checkmarks in the boxes that represent the activities they are most interested in completing. As teaching continues over the next 2 weeks, activities chosen and completed should make a column or a row. When students complete this pattern, they will have completed one activity from three different objectives.
- 1 week—At the start of the unit, the teacher chooses the three activities he or she feels are most valuable for the students. Stations can be set up in the classroom. These three activities are available for student choice throughout the week, as regular instruction takes place.
- 1–2 days—The teacher chooses an activity from the menu to use with the entire class.

Suggested Forms

- All-purpose rubric
- Proposal forms

Name:_____

The Sun

☐ *Create a Mobile* The sun has many features. Make a mobile that names the parts of the sun with information about each.	☐ *Sing a Song* The sun plays a large role in life on Earth. Make a song or a rap about the sun and its importance in our daily lives.	☐ *Write a Story* Using your imagination and what you know about the sun and its impact on Earth, write a story that tells about the day the sun stopped shining. What caused it to stop shining? Describe the days following and what happened on Earth.
☐ *Write a Play* The sun is a star. All stars go through a life cycle. Write a play that shows what might happen to our life on Earth if the sun began to cool down.	☐ **Free Choice** (Fill out your proposal form before beginning the free choice!)	☐ *Draw a Comic Strip* Create a comic strip in which the sun tells about how important it is to Earth's survival.
☐ *Prepare a Speech* Scientists say that the sun affects our daily communication through solar flares. Research this phenomenon and develop your own ideas on how they affect us. Write a report or prepare a speech with your information.	☐ *Present a News Report* News flash! Scientists fear the sun will begin its red giant phase within a year. Present a news report on what this means for the people on Earth.	☐ *Make a Model* Using a medium of your choice, make a three-dimensional model of the sun and label its parts.

Check the boxes you plan to complete. They should form a tic-tac-toe across or down. All products are due by: _____.

The Lunar Cycle

2-5-8 Menu

Objectives Covered Through This Menu and These Activities
* Students will describe the phases of the lunar cycle.
* Students will explain why the lunar cycle appears as it does.

Materials Needed by Students for Completion
* Coat hangers (for mobile)
* Index cards (for mobile)
* String (for mobile)
* Various materials for the lunar cycle model
* Materials for lesson on the lunar cycle

Special Notes on the Use of This Menu
Students have two opportunities to teach the class on this menu. Some students may choose to create a way to act out the lunar cycle. By having students share this information and practice the actions, they will remember the information for later assessments. Students may also choose to prepare a lesson that teaches the lunar cycle. This is a wonderful opportunity for students to hear this important information presented again in a different manner.

Time Frame
* 1–2 weeks—Students are given the menu as the unit is started, and the teacher discusses all of the product options on the menu. As the different options are discussed, students will choose products that add to a total of 10 points. As the lessons progress through the week, the teacher and students refer back to the options associated with the content being taught.
* 1–2 days—The teacher chooses an activity from the menu to use with the entire class.

Suggested Forms
* All-purpose rubric
* Student-taught lesson rubric

The Lunar Cycle

Directions: Choose two activities from the menu below. The activities must total 10 points. Place a checkmark next to each box to show which activities you will complete. All activities must be completed by

_____.

---

2 Points

❏ Make a mobile that shows the different phases in the lunar cycle.

❏ Make a folded book quiz for the lunar cycle. It should focus on the different phases and their order.

---

5 Points

❏ Create an informational newspaper article about the moon and the changes we see from the Earth.

❏ Design a working model to demonstrate the lunar cycle.

❏ Your little sister was observing the night sky and panicked. Although the sky was clear and she could see stars, the moon was gone. Prepare a calm response for your sister, explaining why she may not see the moon right now.

❏ Develop a way to act out the phases of the lunar cycle. Teach your actions to the class.

---

8 Points

❏ Prepare a lesson to teach your classmates about the lunar cycle.

❏ Write a legend about why the moon appears to change each month.

CHAPTER 8

Scientists and the Tools They Use

Tools Scientists Use

Tic-Tac-Toe Menu

Objectives Covered Through This Menu and These Activities

- Students will research the development of microscopes and hand lens.
- Students will analyze common errors associated with using certain tools such as microscopes, thermometers, and balances.
- Students will be able to accurately measure using a graduated cylinder, a triple beam balance, and a meter stick.
- Students will demonstrate proper use of a microscope, hand lens, balance, thermometer, and meter stick.

Materials Needed by Students for Completion

- Hand lens
- Triple beam balance
- Thermometer
- Graduated cylinder
- Microscope
- Video camera (for proper use video)
- Poster board or large white paper

Time Frame

- 2 weeks—Students are given the menu as the unit is started. As the teacher presents lessons throughout the week, he or she should refer back to the options associated with that content. The teacher will go over all of the options for that content and have students place checkmarks in the boxes that represent the activities they are most interested in completing. As teaching continues over the next 2 weeks, activities chosen and completed should make a column or a row. When students complete this pattern, they will have completed one activity from three different objectives.
- 1 week—At the start of the unit, the teacher chooses the three activities he or she feels are most valuable for the students. Stations can be set up in the classroom. These three activities are available for student choice throughout the week, as regular instruction takes place.
- 1–2 days—The teacher chooses an activity from the menu to use with the entire class.

Suggested Forms

- Lab report rubric
- All-purpose rubric
- Proposal forms

Name:_____

Tools Scientists Use

☐ *Prepare a Presentation* Research who developed the first hand lens and microscope. Prepare a presentation that tells about the scientist(s) and how these discoveries took place.	☐ *Create a Poster* Create a common error lab poster for microscopes, goggles, thermometers, and balances. For each of the instruments, record at least two things that could cause a student to use the instrument incorrectly.	☐ *Design an Experiment* Design an experiment with a lab report that could be used with first graders to show how to use science equipment safely.
☐ *Design an Experiment* Design an experiment with a lab report to show the steps that can be used to identify a mystery object using scientific instruments.	☐ **Free Choice** (Fill out your proposal form before beginning the free choice!)	☐ *Create a Brochure* Create an informational brochure for common lab equipment with a picture of each and a description of its specific purpose. Include microscopes, goggles, thermometers, meter sticks, graduated cylinders, and balances.
☐ *Prepare a Video* Prepare a video that shows how to properly use a microscope, hand lens, balance, thermometer, and meter stick.	☐ *Design an Experiment* Design an experiment that teaches others how to use a balance correctly.	☐ *Product of Your Choice* In your opinion, which scientific tool has had the greatest impact on science? Create a product of your choice that shows your decision and gives reasons for your viewpoint.

Check the boxes you plan to complete. They should form a tic-tac-toe across or down. All products are due by: _____.

Young Scientists

Tic-Tac-Toe Menu

Objectives Covered Through This Menu and These Activities
- Students will brainstorm characteristics of scientists.
- Students will compare themselves with well-known scientists.
- Students will realize that they can be scientists.

Materials Needed by Students for Completion
- Magazines (for collage)
- Poster board or large white paper

Special Notes on the Use of This Menu
This unit can be used at anytime throughout the year. Teachers could assign the entire menu for 2 weeks and have it overlap current instruction. It also could be a semester-long menu in which every 6 weeks another product chosen from the menu is due.

Time Frame
- 2 weeks—Students are given the menu as the unit is started. As the teacher presents lessons throughout the week, he or she should refer back to the options associated with that content. The teacher will go over all of the options for that content and have students place checkmarks in the boxes that represent the activities they are most interested in completing. As teaching continues over the next 2 weeks, activities chosen and completed should make a column or a row. When students complete this pattern, they will have completed one activity from three different objectives.
- 1 week—At the start of the unit, the teacher chooses the three activities he or she feels are most valuable for the students. Stations can be set up in the classroom. These three activities are available for student choice throughout the week, as regular instruction takes place.
- 1–2 days—The teacher chooses an activity from the menu to use with the entire class.

Suggested Forms
- All-purpose rubric
- Proposal forms

Young Scientists

☐ *Create a Collage* Use magazines and newspapers to create a collage of words that you feel represent scientists.	☐ *Create a Questionnaire* Choose 10 characteristics of scientists. Create a questionnaire with at least 10 questions that can be used with your classmates to discern whether they share the same characteristics as scientists.	☐ *Write a Letter* Evaluate whether you consider yourself to be a scientist, and write a letter to your teacher explaining your thoughts about this. Include details and specific examples for why you feel this way.
☐ *Write a Biography* You have been contracted to write a biography for one of your classmates, who is a scientist at a young age. Write the biography, describing what he or she studies and what makes that person a successful scientist.	☐ **Free Choice** (Fill out your proposal form before beginning the free choice!)	☐ *Design a Book Cover* You have been contracted to write a biography for one of your classmates, a scientist at an early age. Assuming the book has already been written, design a book cover for it and title it appropriately.
☐ *Make a Venn Diagram* Draw a Venn diagram to compare and contrast yourself with a well-known scientist of your choice.	☐ *Be the Teacher* Science teachers are always saying that all of their students are scientists. Pretend you are a science teacher. In a speech, defend the statement that all of your students are scientists.	☐ *Draw . . .* Using a large piece of paper, draw a picture of a scientist. Incorporate at least 10 characteristics of this scientist into your drawing.

Check the boxes you plan to complete. They should form a tic-tac-toe across or down. All products are due by: _____.

Famous Scientists

Tic-Tac-Toe Menu

Objectives Covered Through This Menu and These Activities
- Students will research scientists important to the current unit of study.
- Students will investigate why scientists are famous.

Materials Needed by Students for Completion
- Microsoft PowerPoint or other slideshow software
- Video camera (optional for news report)
- Scrapbooking materials
- Blank index cards (for trading cards)
- Poster board or large white paper

Special Notes on the Use of This Menu
This unit can be used at anytime throughout the year. Tasks are stated in such a way that students can complete any product within their current unit of study. Teachers can assign the entire menu for 2 weeks and have it overlap current instruction. Another option it to use it as a semester-long menu in which every 6 weeks another product is due. Teachers could also use the entire menu if they wanted to use the entire year to learn about famous scientists.

Time Frame (Short Term)
- 1–2 days—The teacher chooses an activity from the menu to use with the entire class.

Suggested Forms
- All-purpose rubric
- Proposal forms

Name:_____

Famous Scientists

☐ *Design a Windowpane* After folding a piece of paper into six boxes, choose six scientists that are important to our current unit of study. Record the scientists' names and three facts about each in each windowpane.	☐ *Create a Scrapbook* Choose one scientist from our unit of study that most interests you. Create a scrapbook about this scientist's life and accomplishments.	☐ *You Be the Star!* Research one scientist from our present unit of study. Prepare a "You Be the Person" presentation for your class.
☐ *Create a PowerPoint Presentation* Choose one significant scientist from our current unit of study. Create a PowerPoint presentation to accompany a speech on your chosen scientist and his or her contributions to science.	☐ **Free Choice** (Fill out your proposal form before beginning the free choice!)	☐ *Write a Newspaper Article* You have been asked to research a famous scientist from our current unit of study. Write a newspaper article containing the information you locate about the scientist and his or her discoveries.
☐ *Perform a News Report* A scientist from our current unit of study is being nominated for the "Scientist Hall of Fame." Prepare a news report on the scientist and why he or she is qualifying for this special honor.	☐ *Design a Book Cover* There is a new biography being written about a well-known scientist from our current unit. Design a book cover for this scientist's biography and include a creative title.	☐ *Create Trading Cards* Create a set of trading cards for at least 10 scientists who did research or had discoveries in the area we are currently studying.

Check the boxes you plan to complete. They should form a tic-tac-toe across or down. All products are due by: _____.

References

Anderson, L. (Ed.), Krathwohl, D. (Ed.), Airasian, P., Cruikshank, K., Mayer, R., Pintrich, P., et al. (2001). *A taxonomy for learning, teaching, and assessing: A revision of Bloom's taxonomy of educational objectives* (Complete ed.). New York: Longman.

Keen, D. (2001). *Talent in the new millennium: Report on year one of the programme.* Retrieved November 27, 2006, from http://www.dce.ac.nz/research/content_talent.htm

About the Author

After living in the small town of Roscommon, MI, and attending Grand Valley State University, Laurie met a goal she set for herself during her freshman year of high school and began her teaching career by teaching science overseas for 5 years in American schools in both Mexico and Brazil. After returning to the U.S., she taught middle school advanced-level science for 9 years in Houston, TX, before taking a position in the school district's gifted office as a master teacher. This is where she found her true calling—working with the teachers of gifted students; presenting practical, hands-on staff development; and helping teachers develop lessons that better meet the academic needs of gifted children. Currently, she is a full-time independent gifted and science education consultant, traveling throughout the state of Texas and providing staff development for teachers of the gifted and administrators, as well as helping school districts meet their science needs.